Giada's kitchen

Giada's kitchen
New Italian Favorites

giada de laurentiis

photographs by tina rupp

Clarkson Potter/Publishers
New York

Library of Congress Cataloging-in-Publication Data
De Laurentiis, Giada.
    Giada's kitchen : new Italian favorites / Giada De Laurentiis ;
photographs by Tina Rupp. — 1st ed.
        p. cm.
    Includes index.
    1. Cookery, Italian.   I. Title.
    TX723.D3275 2008
    641.5945—dc22
2008005004

ISBN 978-0-307-34659-9

Printed in the United States of America

Design by Wayne Wolf/Blue Cup Creative

10 9 8 7 6 5 4 3 2 1

First Edition

To all my fans,

new and old. Enjoy

and buon appetito!

—gdl

Contents

Introduction

Few things in life give me more pleasure than food, whether eating or cooking for the people I love. And I've always known that somehow, some way, I would find my calling in the food world. For obvious reasons, I felt most comfortable around Italian food; it's what I grew up loving. But I never (ever!) imagined that this love would lead to an opportunity to share my passion for Italian cooking, and my ideas about what Italian food can and *should* be, with so many people. When I made my earliest appearances on Food Network, there were plenty of well-established authorities who had already made their marks on the culinary landscape. I wondered at first what on earth I could bring to the table. Where would I fit in? What new message did I have to share? When I thought about my roots, though, the way my family has always cooked, and the places and people whose food continues to inspire me today, the recipes and ideas began to come. And they haven't stopped since.

For the past five years I have been on a wonderful journey. On my Food Network shows and in my cookbooks I've had the chance to explore every facet of Italian cooking: traditional, seasonal, regional, contemporary, whimsical, and much more. All the while, my own style of cooking has been evolving. From the old recipes of my grandmother's that I still adore, like her verdure al forno and hearty lamb stew with cipollini onions and potatoes, to some of the more updated dishes you'll find in this book, I've found the things that make a recipe just taste *right* to me.

These days, my palate responds most to clean, vibrant, simple flavors, and my eyes can't resist the undeniable freshness of great ingredients and bursts of bright colors. The recipes you'll find in this book represent a nice balance of exciting and healthy dishes; they're hearty but not overwhelming (and a few are moderately sinful because everyone needs a treat once in a while). And because we eat first with our eyes, I made sure that every dish is as beautiful on the plate as it is delicious.

In response to the countless requests I have received from parents who enjoy cooking with their children (or whose kids love to cook themselves), I have also included a chapter just for kids, with easier recipes full of the flavors kids can't resist. The Orecchiette with Mini Chicken Meatballs is one of my favorites (and the recipe

makes about seventy of the little meatballs, so you'll have plenty of leftovers and happy campers).

These recipes reflect what my readers and viewers have told me they are looking for in the meals they prepare, dishes I know will always be well received. They represent five years of lessons I've learned as well as those I have shared since beginning my *Everyday Italian* journey. I've never forgotten that cooking and eating are a shared experience, and my goal as a chef is to ensure that each "everyday" experience is a memorable one for you and your family. I hope you will find some new favorites here, as well as a few "shining moments" that will linger in your memory. xo

Giada

Appetizers
and First Courses

FRESH TOMATO AND GOAT CHEESE STRATA WITH HERB OIL

RED PEPPER CHEESECAKE

PECORINO ROMANO WITH APPLES AND FIG JAM

MEDITERRANEAN BRUSCHETTA

TUSCAN MUSHROOMS

TOMATO, WATERMELON, AND BASIL SKEWERS

CRISPY SMOKED MOZZARELLA WITH HONEY AND FIGS

CROSTATA WITH MUSHROOMS AND PANCETTA

CROSTATA WITH APPLES, WALNUTS, AND GORGONZOLA

GARLIC AND SUN-DRIED TOMATO CORN MUFFINS

OLIVE OIL MUFFINS

PECORINO CRACKERS

APPLE AND THYME MARTINI

THYME SIMPLE SYRUP

POMEGRANATE AND CRANBERRY BELLINIS

SIMPLE SYRUP

AMARETTO SOUR WITH PROSECCO

APPETIZERS
AND FIRST COURSES

For some reason, many people find appetizers the most intimidating course of the meal to put together. Most simply resort to store-bought cocktail nibbles or perhaps a plate of fruit and cheese or crudités with dips, but the possibilities are so much more interesting than those tired standbys. Both in America and in Italy, the purpose of an appetizer or a first course is the same: to whet the appetite for the meal to come without being too heavy or filling. In Italy, of course, the antipasto is generally the first of five courses, but few Americans subscribe to this kind of drawn-out meal unless it's a very special occasion. That doesn't mean, though, that you can't take a page out of the Italians' book. I like to blend Italian and American traditions with appetizers that can work either as the first course of a more formal meal or be passed at a cocktail party as an hors d'oeuvre. They are uniformly simple to make (many of them in advance) but they look very impressive, and their vibrant colors and flavors will have everyone eager for the meal to come.

Fresh Tomato and Goat Cheese Strata with Herb Oil

For entertaining I usually prefer dishes that can be made ahead of time, but I make an exception for this one. It does need to be assembled at the last minute; but when you want something particularly beautiful to start a small dinner party, it's worth the extra effort. The flavor of mint really shines through and the colors are stunning together, especially if you use a mix of heirloom tomato varieties.

4 to 6 servings

Goat Cheese Filling
- 8 ounces goat cheese, at room temperature
- ¼ cup heavy cream
- Pinch of salt and freshly ground black pepper
- 1 cup walnut pieces
- 3 ripe tomatoes, cored and sliced ½ to ¾ inch thick

Herb Oil
- ¾ cup fresh mint leaves
- ¾ cup fresh basil leaves
- 1 cup olive oil
- Pinch of salt and freshly ground black pepper

To make the filling, combine the goat cheese and cream in a medium bowl and beat together using an electric mixer until light and fluffy. Season with salt and pepper.

To make the herb oil, combine the herbs in a food processor and pulse a few times to chop them. With the machine running, add the oil in a slow stream and process until very smooth with visible flecks of the herbs remaining. Season with salt and pepper and combine, then transfer the oil to a small bowl, cover with plastic wrap, and set aside.

Toast the walnuts in a small, dry skillet over medium heat until they begin to darken slightly and are fragrant. (You can also toast them on a rimmed baking sheet in a 350°F oven for about 10 minutes.) Transfer the nuts to a cutting board to cool slightly, then chop them coarsely.

Place half the tomato slices on serving plates and top each with a spoonful of the goat cheese mixture. Top each with a second tomato slice and another spoonful of the rest of the goat cheese filling. Drizzle the strata with some of the herb oil, and sprinkle with the walnuts.

Note: Leftover oil can be stored in a covered container in the refrigerator; it will remain flavorful for a day or two. Use it to drizzle on grilled fish and vegetables, on pasta, and in salad dressings for an extra herbal punch.

Red Pepper Cheesecake

Despite the apricot topping, this is a savory dish, not a dessert, and it's a knockout addition to an appetizer buffet. Be sure to pat the bell peppers dry with paper towels and don't chop them too fine or they will turn the cheese filling pink. Note that the pan size is a bit unusual so make sure you have the right one before you start the recipe.

4 to 6 servings

4 ounces ricotta cheese, at room temperature
4 ounces cream cheese, at room temperature
2 ounces goat cheese, at room temperature
1 tablespoon sugar
1 egg
Kosher salt
2 jarred roasted red bell peppers cut in thin strips and halved (about ½ cup)
4 pitas
2 tablespoons olive oil
Freshly ground black pepper
¼ cup apricot jam
1 to 2 teaspoons hot water

Preheat the oven to 350°F. Wrap the outside of a 4½-inch round springform pan with 2 layers of heavy-duty foil.

Place the ricotta, cream cheese, and goat cheese in a food processor and pulse to mix. Add the sugar, egg, and a pinch of salt and pulse a few times until well mixed and thick and creamy. Fold in the red pepper strips with a rubber spatula. Pour the cheese mixture into the springform pan.

Place the springform pan in a roasting pan and pour enough hot water into the roasting pan to come halfway up the sides of the springform pan. Bake until the cheesecake is golden at the edges and the center of the cake moves slightly when the pan is gently shaken, about 45 minutes (the cake will become firm when it is cold). Transfer the cake to a wire rack to cool for 1 hour. Refrigerate until the cheesecake is cold, at least 3 hours and up to 2 days.

To make the pita chips, preheat the oven to 350°F.

Cut the pitas into 8 triangles each (like a pie). Place the triangles on rimmed baking sheets. Drizzle the triangles with the olive oil and sprinkle with salt and pepper. Bake until crisp and golden, about 12 to 15 minutes.

To serve, combine the jam and the hot water in a small bowl and stir until the jam is liquefied. Remove the cheesecake from the springform pan and place on a serving plate. Drizzle the jam mixture over the top of the cheesecake. Serve the pita chips alongside.

Pecorino Romano
with Apples and Fig Jam

Here's why I love this dish: it looks gorgeous on the plate, and it's much more sophisticated than the simplicity of the ingredients would suggest. It's a two-biter with lots of strong layers of flavor: first the bite of the cheese, then the crisp lemony tang of the apple and the sweet jammy aftertaste of the figs. Together, the combination is amazing. Use the fig jam on anything from pancakes to pork chops.

4 to 6 servings

6 dried figs, halved
½ cup Simple Syrup (page 38)
2 tablespoons brandy
¼ cup chopped toasted hazelnuts (see Note)
24 baguette slices
Olive oil, for drizzling
½ cup freshly grated Pecorino Romano cheese
1 large apple (Granny Smith or Braeburn)
¼-pound chunk Pecorino Romano cheese, for shaving 24 pieces

Note: To toast the nuts, heat them in a small, dry heavy-bottomed skillet over medium heat until they are fragrant and lightly toasted, 8 to 10 minutes. Spread the nuts on a baking sheet to cool completely before using.

Preheat the oven to 375°F.

Combine the figs, simple syrup, and brandy in a small saucepan. Bring the mixture to a simmer over medium heat, then turn off the heat and set aside for 10 minutes to plump the figs and cool slightly. Transfer the fig mixture to a food processor. Add the hazelnuts and blend, pulsing a few times, until puréed. Set aside.

Place the baguette slices on a heavy baking sheet and drizzle with olive oil. Top each slice with 1 teaspoon of the grated Pecorino Romano. Bake until the bread is toasted and the cheese is melted and golden, about 7 minutes.

Quarter the apple and slice off the cores. Cut each quarter into 6 thin slices.

Top each toast slice with 2 teaspoons of the fig jam, a slice of apple, and a piece of shaved Pecorino Romano. Transfer the toasts to a platter and serve.

Mediterranean Bruschetta

Most Italians would have all these ingredients readily at hand in their pantry; in fact, it's what my mother fixed for me and my siblings as an after-school snack. I've updated it a bit with fresh mint to make a snappy appetizer bite.

Makes about 16; 4 to 6 servings

Bread

1 pound ciabatta loaf, cut into ½-inch-thick slices (about 16)
¼ cup olive oil
Juice of 1 lemon (about 3 tablespoons)
1 teaspoon dried oregano
Salt and freshly ground black pepper

Topping

1 (15-ounce) container whole-milk ricotta cheese
2 large tomatoes, cored, seeded, and diced (about 2 cups)
3 tablespoons finely chopped fresh mint leaves, plus more for garnish
½ teaspoon salt
¼ teaspoon freshly ground black pepper

Place a grill pan over medium-high heat or preheat a gas or charcoal grill. Drizzle the bread slices with olive oil. Grill the bread until golden on both sides, 2 to 3 minutes per side. Remove the bread to a plate and squeeze the lemon juice over the bread slices. Sprinkle the bread slices with the dried oregano, salt, and pepper.

In a medium bowl combine the ricotta, tomatoes, mint, salt, and pepper. Stir gently to combine.

To serve, either spoon the cheese topping onto the bread and sprinkle with more chopped mint, or place the cheese topping in a bowl garnished with the mint and serve with the grilled bread alongside.

Tuscan Mushrooms

If you think stuffed mushrooms are bland, you'll find these a welcome change of pace: the flavors are quite robust. These are equally good right out of the oven or at room temperature, and they make a nice hors d'oeuvre option for non-meat-eaters.

4 to 6 servings

½ cup diced jarred roasted red bell peppers
½ cup diced pitted green olives
½ cup freshly grated Pecorino Romano
2 scallions, white parts only, finely chopped
2 tablespoons extra-virgin olive oil
½ teaspoon salt
¼ teaspoon freshly ground black pepper
1 pound white button mushrooms, cleaned and stemmed
¼ cup finely chopped fresh basil leaves

Preheat the oven to 400°F. Line a rimmed baking sheet with parchment paper.

In a medium bowl, mix together the roasted red bell peppers, olives, cheese, scallions, olive oil, salt, and pepper.

On the baking sheet, arrange the mushrooms, gill side up. Spoon the filling into the mushroom cavities, mounding it slightly. Bake until the mushrooms are tender, about 20 minutes.

Transfer the mushrooms to a serving platter, sprinkle with the chopped basil, and serve.

Tomato, Watermelon, and Basil Skewers

Everyone seems to love this simple combination of clean, fresh flavors. If watermelon is not in season you can substitute cantaloupe, but for a burst of pure flavor that really plays off the herbal flavor of the tomatoes, you can't beat watermelon. Stacking the skewers vertically and serving them upright looks especially elegant.

6 to 8 servings

¼ cup balsamic vinegar
¼ cup sugar
1 4- to 5-pound seedless watermelon
60 small basil leaves (or torn larger leaves)
16 cherry tomatoes, halved
2 tablespoons extra-virgin olive oil
Coarse or kosher salt

Special equipment: 16 (6-inch) wooden skewers

Combine the balsamic vinegar and sugar in a small nonreactive saucepan. Bring to a simmer over medium heat, stirring occasionally, until the sugar is dissolved. Remove from the heat and set aside to cool.

Cut the top and bottom off the watermelon, then make 4 straight cuts down the sides so you have a cube of rindless watermelon. Cut the cube into 1½-inch slices, then cut the slices into 1½-inch cubes. Assemble the skewers by pushing a basil leaf to the end of one skewer. Then skewer a cube of watermelon, then a tomato half. Continue with another watermelon cube, basil leaf, and tomato half, ending with a basil leaf. Repeat to make 15 more skewers.

Drizzle the skewers with the reserved balsamic syrup and the olive oil. Sprinkle with salt. Serve.

Crispy Smoked Mozzarella with Honey and Figs

Honestly, there's not much that's better than fried mozzarella with something sweet drizzled on top. In Santorini I tasted a dish like this, but made with feta; here I've substituted smoked mozzarella, which has a similar salty flavor but is a bit creamier. The smokiness plays off the sweetness of the figs beautifully.

6 servings

6 sheets phyllo dough, defrosted if frozen

6 ounces smoked mozzarella cheese at room temperature, cut into 6 sticks of equal size

Vegetable oil, for deep frying

8 ounces dried figs, stemmed and quartered

¾ cup honey, plus more for drizzling

3 teaspoons black sesame seeds

Unfold the phyllo sheets and place on a dry work surface with a slightly damp towel on top to keep them from becoming brittle. Take out 1 sheet of phyllo and place it vertically on a work surface, with a short edge toward you. Place 1 piece of cheese near the bottom of the sheet. Fold the end up loosely over the cheese, then fold in the sides. Keep folding until you have a tidy package about 3½ x 4 inches. Make 5 more packets with the remaining cheese and phyllo.

In a large pot, heat an inch of vegetable oil to 350°F over medium heat. Fry the phyllo and cheese packages, 2 or 3 at a time, until golden, about 2 minutes per side. Drain on a baking sheet lined with paper towels.

While the cheese packages fry, combine the figs and honey in a small saucepan. Heat over low heat until the honey is warm.

To serve, place 1 cheese package on a plate. Spoon some figs onto each cheese package and drizzle some honey over each serving. Sprinkle with black sesame seeds and serve immediately.

Crostata with Mushrooms and Pancetta

A crostata is a free-form tart that can be served as a dessert or, like these two, filled with savory ingredients as an elegant starter.

4 servings

Pastry Crust

- 1½ cups all-purpose flour
- ½ teaspoon salt
- 3 tablespoons cold unsalted butter, cut into small pieces
- ½ cup mascarpone cheese
- 1½ tablespoons lemon juice
- 3 tablespoons ice water

Mushroom Filling

- 4 tablespoons olive oil
- 2 ounces diced pancetta
- 2 shallots, minced
- 1 pound assorted mushrooms, such as cremini, shiitake, and button
- 1 tablespoon chopped fresh thyme
- ½ teaspoon salt
- ¼ teaspoon freshly ground black pepper
- ⅓ cup (1 ounce) grated smoked mozzarella cheese
- ⅓ cup (1 ounce) grated fontina cheese
- 2 tablespoons freshly grated Parmesan cheese

- 1 large egg, lightly beaten

For the crust: In a food processor combine the flour and salt, and pulse to combine. Add the butter and pulse until the butter is finely chopped and the mixture resembles coarse meal. Add the mascarpone and lemon juice and pulse a few times. Add the ice water and run the machine just until the mixture is moist and crumbly, but do not form a ball. Turn the dough out onto a sheet of plastic wrap and press into a disk. Wrap the dough tightly and refrigerate for 20 minutes.

For the mushroom filling: Heat 2 tablespoons of the olive oil in a large sauté pan over medium-high heat. Add the pancetta and cook until crisp and golden, about 4 minutes. Using a slotted spoon, transfer the cooked pancetta to a small bowl. Add the remaining 2 tablespoons of olive oil to the pan. Add the shallots and cook for 30 seconds. Add the mushrooms and cook, stirring frequently, until all of the moisture has evaporated, about 12 minutes. Remove the pan from the heat and stir in the cooked pancetta along with the fresh thyme, salt, and pepper. Set aside to cool for 10 minutes.

Place an oven rack in the lower third of the oven and preheat the oven to 400°F.

Unwrap the chilled dough and place it on a sheet of parchment paper. Roll the dough into an 11-inch circle, about ¼ inch thick. Lift the parchment paper and transfer it and the dough to the baking sheet.

Stir the mozzarella and fontina into the cooled mushroom filling and spread in the center of the dough circle, leaving a 2-inch border. Sprinkle the filling with the Parmesan. Fold the dough border up over the filling to form an 8-inch round, pleating the edge of the pastry. Brush the crust with the beaten egg.

Bake the crostata until the crust is golden, about 25 minutes. Slice and serve.

Crostata with Apples, Walnuts, and Gorgonzola
4 servings

Apple Filling
   3 tablespoons unsalted butter
   4 small Granny Smith apples, peeled, cored, and cut into ¼-inch slices
   ¼ cup sugar
   ¾ teaspoon ground cinnamon
   1 tablespoon fresh lemon juice
   1 teaspoon grated lemon zest
   ½ cup chopped walnuts
   ⅓ cup crumbled Gorgonzola cheese

   Pastry Crust (opposite) made with 1 tablespoon of sugar added along with the dry ingredients, chilled
   1 large egg, lightly beaten

For the apple filling: Melt the butter in a large nonstick skillet over medium heat. Add the apple slices, sugar, and cinnamon and cook, stirring frequently, for 5 minutes, until the apples are softened but not mushy. Set aside to cool for 10 minutes. Stir in the lemon juice and zest, walnuts, and Gorgonzola cheese.

Place an oven rack in the lower third of the oven and preheat the oven to 400°F.

Unwrap the chilled dough and place it on a sheet of parchment paper. Roll the dough into an 11-inch circle, about ¼ inch thick. Lift the parchment paper and transfer it and the dough to the baking sheet.

Spread the cooled apple filling in the center of the dough circle, leaving a 2-inch border. Fold the dough border up over the filling to form an 8-inch round, pleating the edge of the pastry. Brush the crust with the beaten egg.

Bake the crostata until the crust is golden, about 25 minutes. Cool on the baking sheet for 10 minutes before slicing.

Garlic and Sun-dried Tomato Corn Muffins

I *love* corn muffins, so I'm always looking for new twists on the old standby, which can be kind of bland. These have the surprise of little flecks of sun-dried tomatoes and tender corn kernels, and the garlic makes them so rich they don't need butter or another topping.

Makes 16 muffins

2 (8½-ounce) packages corn muffin
    mix, such as Jiffy
⅔ cup diced sun-dried tomatoes (from
    an 8-ounce jar)
2 cups frozen corn kernels, thawed
3 garlic cloves, minced
⅔ cup buttermilk
⅔ cup sour cream
2 large eggs, beaten

Preheat the oven to 375°F. Insert paper liners in 16 muffin cups or grease the tins.

In a large bowl, combine the corn, muffin mix, garlic, and sun-dried tomatoes. Stir to combine. Mix in the buttermilk, sour cream, and eggs and stir just until combined.

Spoon the mixture into the muffin tins, filling up the cups about halfway. Bake until golden brown on top and a toothpick inserted into the middle of a muffin comes out clean, about 15 minutes.

Olive Oil Muffins

Olive oil in a muffin? It may sound strange, but the first impression you'll get from these muffins is the citrus zests and almonds, not the fruity flavor of the olive oil. What the oil contributes is a more delicate, cakey consistency and a moist, rich texture.

Makes 12 muffins

1¾ cups all-purpose flour
2 teaspoons baking powder
½ teaspoon salt
1 cup granulated sugar
4 large eggs
2 teaspoons grated orange zest
2 teaspoons grated lemon zest
2 tablespoons balsamic vinegar
2 tablespoons whole milk
¾ cup extra-virgin olive oil
⅔ cup sliced almonds, toasted
  (see Note)
Confectioners' sugar, for sifting

Preheat the oven to 350°F. Place paper liners in a 12-cup muffin tin.

In a medium bowl, stir together the flour, baking powder, and salt. Use an electric mixer to beat the granulated sugar, eggs, and zests in a large bowl until pale and fluffy, about 3 minutes. Beat in the vinegar and milk, then gradually beat in the oil. Add the flour mixture and stir by hand just until blended. Crush the almonds with your hands as you add them to the batter and stir until mixed. Fill the muffin tin almost to the top of the paper liners. Bake until golden on top and a tester inserted into the center of a muffin comes out with moist crumbs attached, 20 to 25 minutes. Transfer to a wire rack and cool the muffins in the tin for 10 minutes, then turn the muffins out onto the rack and cool for 5 more minutes. Sift confectioners' sugar over the muffins and serve.

Note: To toast the almonds, spread them on a baking sheet and bake in a 350°F oven for 6 to 8 minutes, stirring once or twice. Watch carefully to keep them from burning.

Pecorino Crackers

There's a lot of flavor in these little crackers, which are the perfect blend of flakey and cheesy. I add these to a bread basket, crumble them over salads, and float them in soup. They keep well in a sealable plastic bag, so make a double batch; you'll find lots of ways to use them.

Makes 24 crackers

1¼ cups freshly grated Pecorino Romano
½ teaspoon salt
¼ teaspoon freshly ground black pepper
⅛ teaspoon cayenne pepper
½ cup (1 stick) unsalted butter, at room temperature
1 cup all-purpose flour

Preheat the oven to 350°F. Line 1 or 2 baking sheets with parchment paper.

Combine the cheese, salt, black pepper, and cayenne pepper in a medium bowl and stir to combine. Add the butter. Using a hand mixer, beat the cheese mixture and butter until combined. Add the flour ¼ cup at a time, mixing only until incorporated and the mixture holds together.

Place tablespoon-size balls of the dough on the parchment-lined baking sheets, tapping the dough down gently with your fingertips. Bake until just beginning to brown at the edges, about 15 minutes. Let the crackers cool on the baking sheets for a few minutes, then transfer them to a serving plate.

Apple and Thyme Martini

In Seattle, where I first had a version of this drink, martinis come garnished with a sprig of Douglas fir. Thyme syrup contributes a similar herbaceous zing, and little balls of apple are a whimsical touch. This is a great cocktail.

4 servings

Ice
10 ounces vodka
6 ounces apple juice
¼ cup Thyme Simple Syrup (recipe follows)
1 large apple, peeled
4 fresh thyme sprigs

Chill 4 martini glasses in the freezer.

Fill a cocktail shaker with ice. Add the vodka, apple juice, and thyme syrup and shake for about 10 seconds. Divide among the 4 chilled martini glasses.

Using a melon baller, scoop out small balls of apple. Place 3 balls of apple and 1 sprig of thyme in each glass for garnish. Serve immediately.

Thyme Simple Syrup

Makes 1 cup

1 cup sugar
5 large fresh thyme sprigs

In a saucepan, combine the sugar, thyme, and ½ cup water. Bring to a boil over medium heat, reduce the heat, and simmer until the sugar has dissolved, about 5 minutes. Take the pan off the heat and cool the syrup. Any extra cooled syrup can be saved in an airtight container in the refrigerator for up to 1 week.

Pomegranate and Cranberry Bellinis

Pomegranates and cranberries are both widely available in the fall, making this the perfect cocktail for any holiday party.

8 to 12 servings

1 cup ice
1½ cups Simple Syrup (recipe follows)
1¼ cups pomegranate juice, chilled
1 cup cranberry juice, chilled
1 (750 ml) bottle Prosecco, chilled
2 limes, thinly sliced
1 bunch fresh mint, for garnish
½ cup (2½ ounces) pomegranate
    seeds, for garnish

Special equipment: a 6- to 8-cup
    capacity punch bowl

Place the ice in the punch bowl. Add the Simple Syrup, pomegranate juice, and cranberry juice. Stir well. Slowly pour in the Prosecco. Garnish with lime slices, mint sprigs, and pomegranate seeds and serve.

As an alternative to serving from a punch bowl, make the bellini mixture in a 6- to 8-cup pitcher. Divide the pomegranate seeds between 12 champagne flutes, add 1 slice of lime and 1 sprig of mint to each glass, and pour the bellini mixture into the prepared glasses.

Simple Syrup

Makes 1½ cups

1 cup water
1 cup sugar

In a saucepan, combine the water and sugar over medium heat. Bring to a boil, reduce heat, and simmer for 5 minutes, stirring occasionally, until the sugar has dissolved. Take the pan off the heat and allow the syrup to cool.

Amaretto Sour with Prosecco

4 to 6 servings

½ cup sugar, plus ⅓ cup
    for sugaring the rims
Zest of 1 lime
Zest and juice of 1 lemon,
    plus 1 lemon, halved
3 cups Prosecco
½ cup Amaretto liqueur
Ice cubes
Lemon and lime slices, for garnish

In a small saucepan, combine ½ cup sugar and ¼ cup water. Bring to a boil over medium heat, then simmer over low heat for 5 minutes, stirring occasionally. Let cool, about 20 minutes.

In a shallow bowl, combine the remaining ⅓ cup sugar with the lime and lemon zests. Rub 1 lemon half around the rim of each glass, making sure to coat them evenly both inside and out. Lightly press the rim into the citrus sugar to frost.

In a pitcher, combine the Prosecco, Amaretto, lemon juice, and the cooled syrup. Pour into the sugared glasses over ice.

Garnish each glass with a slice of lemon and a slice of lime.

Soups,
Panini, and Snacks

HEARTY TOMATO SOUP WITH LEMON AND ROSEMARY

TUSCAN WHITE BEAN AND GARLIC SOUP

SPICY CALAMARI STEW WITH GARLIC TOASTS

FISH MINESTRONE WITH HERB SAUCE

PROSCIUTTO AND MELON SOUP

CURRIED CHICKEN SANDWICH WITH RADICCHIO AND PANCETTA

FOCACCIA LOBSTER ROLLS

TALEGGIO AND PEAR PANINI

CROISSANT PANINI

PANINI WITH CHOCOLATE AND BRIE

ARTICHOKE AND TUNA PANINI WITH GARBANZO BEAN SPREAD

CHICKEN AND ORZO FRITTATA

LINGUINE AND PROSCIUTTO FRITTATAS

SPICED AMERICANO WITH CINNAMON WHIPPED CREAM

ICED CAFFÈ LATTE

AMARETTO AND RASPBERRY SMOOTHIE

SOUPS,
PANINI, AND SNACKS

Any food can be a snack, really. This is something I learned growing up when my mom would make frittatas and panini for my sister, brothers, and me to enjoy during the day, especially when we came home from school in the afternoon. These are also the recipes to turn to when the day gets away from you, or you're just not in the mood for a heavy meal. At such times a hearty soup and delicious panini can easily make for a satisfying lunch or dinner—even a breakfast. I have an endless craving for my Panini with Chocolate and Brie, a treat I make when friends drop by but also serve occasionally as a cocktail nibble (cut in quarters) and even for dessert. The Hearty Tomato Soup with Lemon and Rosemary is something else I would eat any time of day, whether between meals or as the main event itself. And for an afternoon pick-me-up, nothing warms me more than Spiced Americano with Cinnamon Whipped Cream.

Hearty Tomato Soup
with Lemon and Rosemary

I made this for an après-ski menu on *Everyday Italian*. It is quite hearty and the beans give it nice body without making it *too* thick. The whipped cream garnish is beautiful and becomes even more fragrant as it slowly melts into the soup.

6 to 8 servings

2 tablespoons unsalted butter
1 onion, peeled and chopped
2 carrots, peeled and chopped
   (about 1 cup)
2 garlic cloves, chopped
1 (15-ounce) can cannellini (white)
   beans, drained and rinsed
1 (28-ounce) can crushed tomatoes
3 cups chicken broth
1 bay leaf
2 teaspoons minced fresh rosemary
½ teaspoon red pepper flakes
¾ teaspoon salt
½ teaspoon freshly ground black pepper
⅔ cup heavy cream
Zest of 1 lemon

In a large soup pot, melt the butter over medium-high heat. Add the onion, carrots, and garlic and cook until the vegetables are tender, about 4 minutes. Add the beans, tomatoes, broth, bay leaf, 1 teaspoon of the rosemary, and the red pepper flakes. Bring the soup to a boil over high heat, then reduce the heat to low and simmer for 30 minutes, covered.

Purée the soup in a blender in batches, being careful to remove and discard the bay leaf. Return the soup to the soup pot and keep warm over low heat. Season with salt and pepper.

In a medium bowl, whip the cream to soft peaks. Fold in the lemon zest and the remaining teaspoon of rosemary. To serve, ladle the soup into bowls and dollop each bowl with the lemon-rosemary whipped cream. Serve immediately.

Tuscan White Bean and Garlic Soup

I love the versatility of cannellini beans. I've puréed them to make a dip and have used them as a thickener for soups. They've made many appearances in salads and even pasta dishes. This time, though, the cannellini bean is the star, offering a creamy, buttery texture for the base of the soup, which perfectly absorbs the flavors of the aromatics.

4 to 6 servings

2 tablespoons unsalted butter
1 tablespoon olive oil
2 shallots, chopped
2 sage leaves, stems removed
2 (15-ounce) cans cannellini beans, rinsed and drained
4 garlic cloves, peeled and halved
4 cups low-sodium chicken broth
½ cup heavy cream
½ teaspoon salt
½ teaspoon freshly ground black pepper
6 slices ciabatta bread
Extra-virgin olive oil, for drizzling

Place a medium, heavy soup pot over medium heat. Add the butter, olive oil, and shallots. Cook, stirring occasionally, until the shallots are softened, about 3 minutes. Add the sage leaves, cannellini beans, and garlic and stir to combine. Add the chicken broth to the pan. Bring the mixture to a simmer and cook gently until the garlic is softened, about 15 minutes. Pour half of the soup into a large bowl. Carefully ladle a third to half of the soup from the bowl into a blender or food processor and purée until smooth (be careful to hold the top of the blender tightly, as hot liquids expand when they are blended). Pour the blended soup back into the pot and repeat with the remaining soup from the bowl. Once all the soup is returned to the soup pot, stir in the cream, salt, and pepper. Cover and keep warm over very low heat.

Place a grill pan over medium-high heat. Drizzle the slices of ciabatta bread with the extra-virgin olive oil. Grill the bread until it is warm and golden grill marks appear, about 3 minutes per side. Serve the soup in bowls with the grilled bread alongside.

Spicy Calamari Stew with Garlic Toasts

If you love fried calamari, you'll really like having a new way to serve squid. The soup is thicker than a cioppino but not quite a chowder, and it's nice and light. My husband, Todd, loves this soup because it's spicy and the calamari gives it a meaty quality. Don't add the calamari until right before you're ready to serve, though, or it will become rubbery.

4 to 6 servings

Calamari Stew

- 3 tablespoons olive oil
- 4 garlic cloves, peeled and halved
- 2 cups dry white wine
- 2 (15-ounce) cans tomato sauce
- 2 teaspoons chopped fresh thyme leaves
- 2 teaspoons red pepper flakes
- 1 teaspoon salt
- 1 teaspoon freshly ground black pepper
- 2 pounds calamari (squid), bodies thinly sliced, tentacles whole

Garlic Toast

- 4 to 6 slices of rustic Italian bread
- Olive oil, for drizzling
- 2 to 3 whole garlic cloves, peeled

Preheat the oven to 350°F.

Warm the olive oil over low heat in a medium pot. Add the garlic and cook, stirring frequently, until fragrant, about 2 minutes. Increase the heat to medium. Slowly add the white wine and cook for 1 minute, then add the tomato sauce, thyme, red pepper flakes, salt, and pepper. Bring the mixture to a simmer and cook for 8 minutes. Stir in the calamari and continue to cook just until the mixture comes back to a simmer and the squid is opaque, about 2 more minutes.

While the stew simmers, drizzle the bread slices with olive oil. Toast until the bread is crisp and turning golden brown, 8 to 10 minutes. Remove from the oven and rub the top of the toasts with the whole garlic cloves. Serve immediately with the calamari stew.

Fish Minestrone with Herb Sauce

In Venice you'll find this soup in nearly every restaurant, and every version is a little bit different. I use two kinds of beans because I like the different textures each contributes: the cannellini are creamy while the garbanzos (chickpeas) have a slightly firmer bite. The final herb sauce brightens and freshens the long-cooked flavors.

You can substitute any mild white fish for the snapper, but try to keep the fillets whole as the soup cooks. I always feel if I've spent the money for a beautiful piece of fish, I want people to see it, not just find tiny flakes throughout the soup.

4 to 6 servings

2 tablespoons olive oil
2 leeks (white parts only), thinly sliced (about 1 cup)
2 carrots, peeled and thinly sliced (about 1 cup)
2 zucchini, trimmed and thinly sliced (about 2 cups)
1 cup bite-size pieces of green beans
1 cup canned garbanzo beans, rinsed and drained
1 cup canned cannellini beans, rinsed and drained
6 cups low-sodium chicken broth
4 to 6 (6-ounce) snapper fillets
1 teaspoon salt
½ teaspoon freshly ground black pepper

Herb Sauce

2 cups fresh flat-leaf parsley leaves
¼ cup fresh oregano leaves
1 garlic clove
1 tablespoon red wine vinegar
½ cup extra-virgin olive oil
½ teaspoon salt
¼ teaspoon freshly ground black pepper

For the fish minestrone: Warm the olive oil in a large pot over medium-low heat. Add the leeks, carrots, zucchini, and green beans. Stir to combine and cook until tender, about 10 minutes. Add the beans and the chicken broth. Cook until the broth is simmering and the beans are warmed through, about 5 minutes. Season the fish fillets with the salt and pepper and add them to the simmering soup. Simmer until the fish is cooked, about 7 minutes depending on the thickness of the fish. Season the soup with salt and pepper.

For the herb sauce: While the fish cooks, combine the parsley, oregano, garlic, and red wine vinegar in a food processor. Pulse the machine until the herbs are almost a paste. Add the olive oil in a steady stream while the machine is running. Add the salt and pepper.

To serve, ladle the soup into bowls and top each serving with a spoonful of the herb sauce. Serve immediately.

Prosciutto and Melon Soup

After tomato, basil, and mozzarella, prosciutto and melon just might be *the* most classic Italian flavor combination of all time. It gets a whole new lease on life, though, when served as a savory cold soup. The tomato contributes a bit of acidity that tones down the melon's natural sweetness, and salty prosciutto makes the whole dish sing. If you can't find canned San Marzano tomatoes, which are a bit sweeter than regular canned plum tomatoes, go for an organic brand such as Muir Glen.

4 servings

10 slices prosciutto
1 cantaloupe, cut into chunks (about 5 cups)
1 (14-ounce) can San Marzano tomatoes with their juices
½ teaspoon salt
¼ teaspoon freshly ground black pepper
6 fresh basil leaves, very thinly sliced

Preheat the oven to 350°F.

Place the prosciutto slices on a foil-lined baking sheet and bake until firm, golden around the edges, and almost crisp, about 18 minutes. Set aside to cool while you make the soup.

Place half the melon in a blender with half the tomatoes. Pulse the blender until the mixture is puréed. Transfer to a large bowl and purée the remaining melon and tomatoes. Combine both puréed batches in the bowl and season with the salt and pepper.

Ladle the soup into bowls. Crumble the cooled prosciutto crisps over each serving. Sprinkle with the basil and serve.

Curried Chicken Sandwich with Radicchio and Pancetta

Curry powder isn't a traditional Italian ingredient, but over time it has found its way into Italian cuisine simply because of Italy's geographic location and influences from its neighbors. I love the flavorful blend of spices in curry powder, which marries well with mayo and chicken. The radicchio adds a touch of bitterness and the pancetta a perfect crunch.

4 servings

8 ounces thinly sliced pancetta, about 8 slices
½ cup plus 2 tablespoons mayonnaise
1 tablespoon curry powder
1 tablespoon freshly squeezed lime juice
2 teaspoons honey
1½ teaspoons minced peeled fresh ginger
3½ to 4 cups diced roasted chicken (from a 2-pound store-bought roasted chicken)
1½ cups shredded radicchio
4 ciabatta rolls

Fry the pancetta slices in a large skillet over high heat until crispy. Drain the pancetta on paper towels and set aside.

In a large bowl, combine the mayonnaise, curry powder, lime juice, honey, and ginger. Stir to combine. Add the chicken and radicchio and stir to coat with the dressing.

Slice the rolls in half. Spoon the chicken mixture onto the bottom halves of the rolls. Top with pieces of the crispy pancetta and the roll tops and serve.

Focaccia Lobster Rolls

Purists will probably take issue with my spin on lobster rolls, but I think the light, sweet texture of mascarpone enhances the flavor of lobster far better than mayo does. There's no question, though, that this is a decadent dish; enjoy it as an occasional— and outrageously delicious—treat.

4 servings

½ cup mascarpone cheese, at room temperature
¼ cup extra-virgin olive oil
2 tablespoons fresh tarragon leaves
2 tablespoons coarsely chopped fresh chives
Zest of 1 lemon
1 teaspoon fresh lemon juice
1 garlic clove, minced
Salt and freshly ground black pepper
½ pound cooked lobster meat (or diced cooked prawns)
4 focaccia rolls (about 4 by 5 inches each)

In a medium bowl, stir together the mascarpone and olive oil until combined and smooth. Stir in the tarragon, chives, lemon zest, lemon juice, garlic, salt, and pepper.

Cut the lobster meat into nice, big chunks; if using prawns, peel them and cut into 1-inch pieces.

Add the lobster meat to the herb sauce and toss to coat. Divide the lobster mixture among the rolls and serve immediately.

Taleggio and Pear Panini

Use a sweet, ripe (but not overripe) pear such as Bosc or Anjou; if it's not ripe enough, the flavor won't marry with the cheese. Taleggio is a mild, creamy Italian cheese; if you can't find it, Brie is a perfectly fine substitute.

4 servings

1 (1-pound) ciabatta loaf (or 8 slices country bread)
¼ cup olive oil
8 ounces Taleggio cheese, sliced
2 large ripe pears (or apples), cored and cut into ¼-inch wedges
2 tablespoons honey
Pinch of salt
Pinch of freshly ground black pepper
3 ounces arugula or spinach

Note: If you do not have a panini press, you can make the sandwiches in a ridged grill pan. Preheat the grill pan, add the sandwich, then place a weight (a foil-wrapped brick, a smaller skillet with a couple of cans in it) on top. Turn once halfway through.

Preheat a panini press (see Note). Cut the ciabatta loaf into 4 equal pieces. Halve each piece horizontally to make 4 sandwiches. Brush the bread on both sides with olive oil and place the bottom half of the bread slices in the panini press in a single layer. Close the panini press and heat the bread until golden, about 3 to 4 minutes. Repeat with the remaining top slices of bread.

While the top slices of the bread are grilling, begin forming the sandwiches. Divide the cheese among the warm bread. Cover the cheese with slices of fruit. Drizzle the fruit with honey and sprinkle with salt and pepper. Top with a handful of arugula. Place the warmed top half of the bread over the arugula and return the completed sandwich to the panini press for 1 to 2 minutes more to melt the cheese. Cut the sandwiches in half and serve immediately.

Croissant Panini

A hearty yet sophisticated sandwich with enough meat in it to satisfy big appetites. Don't use your stale, leftover croissants for this; you want the butter to melt and crisp up the dough, making it even flakier and completely delicious.

4 servings

4 croissants

4 ounces smoked Gouda cheese, grated (about 1⅓ cups)

8 teaspoons freshly grated Parmesan cheese

4 ounces Genoa salami (about 24 slices)

5 ounces arugula

Heat a panini press. Slice one croissant in half horizontally and place both halves on a work surface, cut side up. Divide ⅓ cup of the smoked Gouda between the top and bottom halves of each croissant, then sprinkle each half with 1 teaspoon of the Parmesan. Top each side with about 3 slices of Genoa salami (about 1 ounce of salami per sandwich, total). Top one half of the sandwich with a small handful of arugula. Close the sandwich and repeat to make 3 more sandwiches. Grill the panini until the cheese melts, 3 to 4 minutes.

Cut each sandwich into thirds. Place the remaining arugula on a serving platter. Place the warm sandwich slices on the arugula. Serve hot.

Panini with Chocolate and Brie

I could eat this sandwich every day for the rest of my life and never get tired of it. The heat of the panini press melts the chocolate and Brie together, and the salty-sweet-gooey goodness that results is my idea of heaven. Sometimes I make these for a cocktail party, cutting each sandwich into four small squares, and it's always a conversation starter.

6 servings

12 slices sourdough bread
⅓ cup extra-virgin olive oil
12 ounces Brie cheese, thinly sliced
1 (12-ounce) bag semisweet chocolate chips
⅓ cup thinly sliced fresh basil leaves

Preheat the panini press.

Brush both sides of the bread with olive oil. Place in the press, close, and grill the bread slices until they begin to turn golden, 1 to 2 minutes. Remove from the panini press and place 2 slices of cheese on one slice of bread, top with ⅓ cup chocolate chips, and sprinkle with basil. Top with another slice of bread. Continue with the remaining sandwiches. Return the sandwiches to the panini press until the chocolate begins to melt, about another 2 minutes.

Cut the sandwiches into 2-inch-wide rectangles or small triangles and transfer to a serving platter.

Artichoke and Tuna Panini with Garbanzo Bean Spread

In Italy the term *panini* refers to any sandwich, whether warm or cold, pressed or not. What makes this different from your average tuna salad sandwich is the garbanzo bean spread; it lends a creamy, earthy flavor that's a thousand times better than any mayonnaise-y sauce and keeps the tuna from tasting dry.

8 servings

Garbanzo Bean Spread
1 (15½-ounce) can garbanzo beans, drained and rinsed
2 garlic cloves
¼ cup fresh mint leaves
2 teaspoons grated lemon zest
3 tablespoons freshly squeezed lemon juice
3 tablespoons extra-virgin olive oil
¼ teaspoon salt
¼ teaspoon freshly ground black pepper

Panini
1 cup pitted black olives, finely chopped
⅔ cup extra-virgin olive oil
½ teaspoon salt
½ teaspoon freshly ground black pepper
2 (5½-ounce) cans Italian tuna in olive oil, drained
1 (13¾-ounce) can quartered artichoke hearts, drained
8 mini baguettes, halved lengthwise
2 cups arugula

For the garbanzo bean spread, combine all the ingredients in a food processor. Pulse until the mixture is smooth. Transfer to a small bowl and set aside.

To make the panini, combine the black olives, olive oil, salt, pepper, tuna, and artichokes in a bowl and toss gently to mix.

Lay out the sliced baguettes. Spread both halves of the baguettes with the garbanzo bean spread. Spoon the tuna mixture onto the bottom half of each sandwich and top with the arugula. Close up the sandwiches. Wrap one end of each sandwich in parchment paper to make it easier to eat, if you like.

Chicken and Orzo Frittata

In this frittata, pasta plays a supporting rather than starring role, giving the eggs a little body. It makes a very pretty, satisfying lunch served with a simple side salad.

4 to 6 servings

¾ cup orzo pasta
6 eggs
⅓ cup whole-milk ricotta cheese
¼ cup crème fraîche
2 cooked chicken breasts, cubed (about 2 cups)
4 scallions, chopped
¼ cup chopped fresh flat-leaf parsley leaves
⅓ cup diced roasted red bell peppers
1 teaspoon salt
¼ teaspoon freshly ground black pepper

Preheat the oven to 375°F. Spray a 1½-quart baking dish with nonstick cooking spray.

Bring a small pot of salted water to a boil over high heat. Add the orzo and cook until tender but still firm to the bite, stirring occasionally, 8 to 10 minutes. Drain the pasta.

In a large bowl, combine the eggs, ricotta, and crème fraîche and stir until the eggs are beaten and the ingredients are thoroughly combined. Add the cooked orzo, chicken, scallions, parsley, red bell peppers, salt, and pepper. Stir to combine.

Pour the mixture into the baking dish and bake for 25 minutes. Turn the oven to broil. Place the baking dish under the broiler until golden brown on top, about 5 minutes. Remove from the oven and let set for 5 minutes before serving. The frittata will settle a bit as it cools.

Linguine and Prosciutto Frittatas

Here's a fun way to use up leftover pasta. When I was young, my mother would throw leftovers of any kind of pasta—red-sauced, white-sauced, whatever—into her frittata mixture for a quick snack for us kids. She generally made one large frittata, but I like to make them in individual servings; that way you can keep them in the fridge and grab one for a quick, nutritious snack, hot or cold.

6 servings

½ pound linguine
7 large eggs
½ cup milk
¼ cup heavy cream
½ cup mascarpone cheese
6 ounces diced prosciutto
5 ounces smoked mozzarella cheese, diced (1 cup diced)
½ cup freshly grated Asiago cheese
¼ cup finely chopped fresh flat-leaf parsley
2 garlic cloves, minced
1 teaspoon salt
¾ teaspoon freshly ground black pepper
⅛ teaspoon freshly grated nutmeg

Bring a large pot of salted water to a boil over high heat. Add the pasta and cook until tender but still firm to the bite, stirring occasionally, 8 to 10 minutes. Drain the pasta in a colander. While the pasta is still in the colander, use kitchen shears to cut the linguine into smaller pieces. The pasta should measure about 3 cups.

Preheat the oven to 375°F. Grease a 12-cup muffin tin.

In a blender, combine the eggs, milk, cream, and mascarpone. Blend until well combined. Transfer the mixture to a large bowl and add the cut pasta, the prosciutto, mozzarella, Asiago, parsley, garlic, salt, pepper, and nutmeg. Stir until the ingredients are combined.

Fill each of the muffin cups with about ⅓ cup of the mixture; both the pasta and liquid should fill the cup almost to the top. Bake until firm and cooked through, 30 to 35 minutes. Let the frittatas cool for 3 minutes before removing from the tin. Arrange on a serving platter or place 2 on each of 6 individual plates and serve.

Spiced Americano with Cinnamon Whipped Cream

When the temperature is particularly frigid, only the promise of a cup of this steaming hot spiced coffee will get me up the mountain for a day of skiing. Fortunately, it is just as inviting on a damp rainy day!

4 servings

1 cup granulated sugar
¼ teaspoon ground allspice
¼ teaspoon ground cinnamon, plus more for dusting
¼ teaspoon ground ginger
1 cup boiling water
1 cup brewed espresso
1 cup heavy cream
2 tablespoons confectioners' sugar

In a small saucepan, combine the granulated sugar and ½ cup water. Bring to a boil over medium heat and reduce the heat to low. Add the allspice, cinnamon, and ginger and simmer for 5 minutes, or until the sugar is dissolved. Take the pan off the heat and set aside.

In a heat-proof pitcher or measuring cup, add the boiling water to the espresso, then divide it among four 6- to 8-ounce cups. Add 2 tablespoons of the spiced syrup to each cup and stir to combine.

Using an electric mixer with a whisk attachment, beat the heavy cream until soft peaks form. Add the confectioners' sugar and continue to beat until stiff. Top each cup of espresso with a dollop of whipped cream. Dust with cinnamon and serve.

Iced Caffè Latte

In the summertime this is a refreshing alternative to iced tea.
I keep the cinnamon syrup in the fridge so when my girlfriends
drop by we have something cool and delicious to sip in the
yard under the hot California sun.

4 servings

4 shots of espresso (about 1½ ounces
  each)
¼ cup Cinnamon Simple Syrup (recipe
  follows)
1⅓ cups whole milk
Crushed ice

Combine the espresso, cinnamon syrup, and
milk in a small pitcher. Fill 4 large, tall glasses
with crushed ice. Pour the latte mixture over
the ice and serve immediately.

Cinnamon Simple Syrup

Makes 1 cup

1 cup sugar
½ cup water
4 cinnamon sticks

In a saucepan combine the sugar, water,
and cinnamon sticks. Bring to a boil over
medium heat, reduce the heat, and simmer
for 5 minutes, or until the sugar has dissolved.
Take the pan off the heat and cool the syrup.
Any extra cooled syrup can be saved in an
airtight container in the refrigerator for up to
one week.

Amaretto and Raspberry Smoothie

As thick and creamy as the richest milkshake, this can also do double duty as a dessert. Serve half portions in pretty stemmed glasses with the cookie crumbles sprinkled on top. Be sure to make this in two batches, because the ingredients will overflow your blender container.

4 servings

12 ounces fresh raspberries (or 12 ounces frozen raspberries, thawed)
1 quart vanilla gelato or ice cream, slightly softened
2 tablespoons almond liqueur such as Amaretto di Sarono
2 teaspoons grated orange zest
Ice
4 amaretti cookies, crushed

Place half the raspberries in a blender with half the gelato, 1 tablespoon of the almond liqueur, and 1 teaspoon of the orange zest. Pulse the blender until the mixture is combined. Add about half a tray of ice cubes and blend until smooth.

Divide the smoothie between 2 highball glasses and make a second batch with the remaining ingredients. Sprinkle some of the crushed cookies over the smoothies and mix them in briefly to distribute. Serve with long spoons and straws.

Salads

and Vegetables

CANTALOUPE, RED ONION, AND WALNUT SALAD

ROMAN SUMMER SALAD

GRILLED EGGPLANT AND GOAT CHEESE SALAD

FENNEL SLAW WITH PROSCIUTTO AND PISTACHIO PESTO

ASPARAGUS AND ZUCCHINI CRUDI

FREGOLA SALAD WITH FRESH CITRUS AND RED ONION

MEDITERRANEAN FARRO SALAD

FARRO WITH COARSE PESTO

PARMESAN POTATO PANCAKE

SPICY PARMESAN GREEN BEANS AND KALE

BROILED ZUCCHINI AND POTATOES WITH PARMESAN CRUST

ARTICHOKE GRATINATA

ASPARAGUS, ARTICHOKE, AND MUSHROOM SAUTÉ WITH TARRAGON VINAIGRETTE

BAKED ARTICHOKES WITH GORGONZOLA AND HERBS

SALADS
AND VEGETABLES

I love salads and veggies, and when done right they can be a completely satisfying meal. I grew up eating lots of salads, though they didn't necessarily involve a big bowl of lettuce. In Italy, a salad can be so many different things, and I've carried that philosophy with me. For me, a good salad incorporates fresh, seasonal, and colorful ingredients; an element of crunch; and a bright dressing to round out the flavors. Sicilians are known for combining local fruits and nuts in their salads, and my Cantaloupe, Red Onion, and Walnut Salad is a good example. In Rome, the salads are more substantial, like an antipasto, and any lettuce is almost an afterthought. For people who don't normally like green veggies, I recommend my Spicy Parmesan Green Beans and Kale, because with the red pepper and Parmesan cheese, it's a dish to make you fall in love with vegetables again.

Cantaloupe, Red Onion, and Walnut Salad

In Sardinia melon, watermelon, and other sweet fruits often find their way into salads. Watermelon is used most commonly, but I find it's easier to get good cantaloupe year-round. This is very fresh tasting and refreshing, and because I always like a little crunch in my salads, I've added some toasted walnuts. Sometimes I add some grated Pecorino cheese to this as well. Serve this after the meal as a palate cleanser before—or instead of—dessert.

4 to 6 servings

Orange Vinaigrette
¼ cup fresh orange juice
1 tablespoon freshly squeezed
   lemon juice
1½ tablespoons raspberry vinegar
3 tablespoons extra-virgin olive oil
Salt and freshly ground black pepper

Salad
1 (3-pound) cantaloupe, cut into
   1-inch cubes
1 small red onion, thinly sliced
2 cups arugula
1 cup chopped walnuts, toasted
   (see Note, page 21)

To make the vinaigrette, combine the orange juice, lemon juice, and raspberry vinegar in a small bowl. Slowly add the olive oil, whisking constantly until the mixture is smooth. Season with salt and pepper to taste.

To make the salad, combine the cantaloupe, red onion, arugula, and ½ cup of the walnuts in a large salad bowl. Pour the dressing over the salad and toss well. Garnish with the remaining walnuts.

Roman Summer Salad

Midway between an antipasto plate and a salad, this is typical of the kind of salads you'll find in Rome, which rarely feature a lot of lettuce. Don't be put off by the anchovies; they are chopped fine and contribute a big kick of flavor and saltiness. Serve it along with a plate of sliced deli meats for a picnic or fall lunch.

4 servings

1 cup balsamic vinegar
1 cup pitted green and black olives, halved
¼ cup chopped fresh flat-leaf parsley leaves
3 anchovy fillets, drained and finely chopped
2 tablespoons capers, rinsed and drained
1 garlic clove, thinly sliced
8 fresh basil leaves, shredded
½ teaspoon freshly ground black pepper
6 tablespoons extra-virgin olive oil
1 pound vine-ripened tomatoes (about 3 tomatoes)

Pour the balsamic vinegar into a small nonreactive saucepan and bring to a boil. Continue to cook over low heat until it is thick, syrupy, and reduced to about ¼ cup, about 20 minutes. Set aside to cool.

Combine the olives, parsley, anchovies, capers, garlic, basil, pepper, and olive oil in a small bowl and toss to combine.

To serve, use a serrated knife to cut the tomatoes into ¼-inch-thick slices. Arrange the tomatoes on a serving plate, overlapping slightly. Spoon the olive and parsley mixture over the tomatoes. Drizzle the balsamic syrup over the salad and serve.

Grilled Eggplant
and Goat Cheese Salad

I always prefer to use Japanese eggplants when I can because I find they are less bitter and don't require salting the way bigger eggplants sometimes do. This is a very substantial salad and also very good looking, with pretty layers of eggplant, cheese, and nuts.

4 to 6 servings

7 Japanese eggplants, ends trimmed,
    cut into 1-inch circles
3 tablespoons olive oil
½ cup pine nuts, toasted (see page 185)
3 ounces goat cheese, crumbled
⅓ cup thinly sliced basil
2 tablespoons chopped fresh mint
    leaves
3 tablespoons extra-virgin olive oil
3 tablespoons balsamic vinegar
½ teaspoon kosher salt
½ teaspoon freshly ground black pepper

Place a grill pan over medium-high heat or preheat a gas or charcoal grill. Place the eggplant slices on a sheet pan or in a large bowl and drizzle with the olive oil; toss to coat with the oil. Grill the eggplant slices until tender and grill marks appear, 3 to 4 minutes per side.

Place the eggplant slices side-by-side on a serving platter. Sprinkle with the pine nuts, goat cheese, basil, and mint. Drizzle with the extra-virgin olive oil and balsamic vinegar, and sprinkle with the salt and pepper.

Fennel Slaw with Prosciutto and Pistachio Pesto

Fennel is best served from fall to spring, when it's in season, and there are a million different ways to take advantage of its crunchy sweetness. Here, the raw bulbs are sliced and dressed with a nutty pistachio pesto and salty bites of prosciutto. The flavors just pair so well together.

4 to 6 servings

Pistachio Pesto
- 2 cups (lightly packed) fresh flat-leaf parsley
- ¾ cup pistachios, toasted (see Note, page 21)
- 1 tablespoon fresh thyme leaves
- 3 garlic cloves
- ¾ cup extra-virgin olive oil
- Salt and freshly ground black pepper

Fennel Slaw
- 4 to 5 fennel bulbs (about 3½ pounds)
- 4 ounces prosciutto, thinly sliced

For the pistachio pesto: Combine the parsley, pistachios, thyme, and garlic cloves in the bowl of a food processor and blend until finely chopped. With the machine running, gradually drizzle in the olive oil, processing until well blended. Season the pesto with salt and pepper to taste.

For the fennel slaw: Trim the tops and bottoms of the fennel bulbs, discarding the stalks and leafy tops. Halve the bulbs and cut out the cores, then slice the bulbs thinly crosswise. Place the sliced fennel in a large serving bowl. Add the pesto and toss to coat well. Tear the prosciutto into 1-inch pieces and add to the bowl. Gently toss to combine.

Asparagus and Zucchini Crudi

It's hard to believe a plate this beautiful is so easy to make. *Crudi* means "raw" and the freshness of raw vegetables is especially welcome as an accompaniment to a heavier pasta. The key to this dish is creating long, graceful ribbons of the raw zucchini; they should look almost like pale green fettuccine noodles.

4 to 6 servings

2 medium zucchini, trimmed
1 bunch of asparagus, trimmed
¼ cup extra-virgin olive oil
2 tablespoons freshly squeezed lemon juice
½ teaspoon salt
¼ teaspoon freshly ground black pepper
1 ounce Pecorino Romano cheese in one chunk

Using a vegetable peeler, shave the zucchini into long thin strips. Thinly slice the asparagus on a diagonal. Put the sliced vegetables in a serving bowl and toss together to combine.

In a small bowl, combine the olive oil, lemon juice, salt, and pepper. Mix well, then drizzle over the vegetables. Toss to coat. Use the vegetable peeler to shave the Pecorino over the salad and serve immediately.

Fregola Salad with Fresh Citrus and Red Onion

Fregola is a toasted semolina pasta that is very popular in Sardinia. You can substitute any small shape pasta, such as orzo, which it resembles, but do make the effort to seek it out at a specialty food shop; its nutty flavor makes this pasta salad really unusual and delicious.

4 to 6 servings

Orange Oil
½ cup extra-virgin olive oil
1 orange, zested

Salad
8 cups low-sodium chicken broth
1 pound fregola pasta (or orzo)
1 orange
1 pink grapefruit
1 small red onion, thinly sliced
½ cup chopped fresh mint leaves
¼ cup chopped fresh basil leaves
½ tablespoon fennel seeds, lightly toasted
1 teaspoon coarse salt
½ teaspoon freshly ground black pepper

To make the orange oil, combine the olive oil and the orange zest in a small bowl and set aside.

To make the salad, in a large saucepan bring the chicken broth to a boil over high heat. Add the pasta and cook until tender but still firm to the bite, stirring occasionally, 10 to 12 minutes. Drain the pasta and dump it onto a large baking sheet. Spread it out into a single layer and let cool for 10 minutes.

Meanwhile, using a small knife, cut all the peel and pith off the orange and grapefruit. Holding the fruit over a large bowl, cut between the membranes to release the segments into the bowl and catch the juices. Add the onion, mint, basil, fennel seeds, salt, pepper, and cooled fregola pasta.

Add the reserved orange oil to the pasta. Toss all the ingredients together and serve.

Mediterranean Farro Salad

This is a hearty meal in a bowl—like an antipasto with the added substance of the earthy grain.

6 side-dish servings

10 ounces farro (about 1½ cups)
2 teaspoons kosher salt
½ pound green beans, trimmed and
    cut into 1- to 2-inch pieces
    (about 2 cups)
½ cup pitted black olives
1 medium red bell pepper, cored,
    seeded, and cut into thin strips
    (about 4 ounces or 1 cup)
3 ounces Parmesan cheese, crumbled
    (about ¾ cup)
¼ cup snipped fresh chives
¼ cup sherry vinegar
¼ cup extra-virgin olive oil
1 tablespoon Dijon mustard
1 teaspoon freshly ground black pepper

In a medium saucepan, combine 4 cups of water with the farro. Bring to a boil over high heat, then cover and simmer over medium-low heat until the farro is almost tender, about 20 minutes. Add 1½ teaspoons of the salt and simmer until the farro is tender, about 10 minutes longer. Drain well. Transfer to a large bowl and let cool.

Meanwhile, bring a medium pot of salted water to a boil over high heat. Add the green beans, stir, and cook for 2 minutes. Drain the green beans, then transfer to a bowl of ice water. Let the beans cool in the water for 2 minutes, then drain well.

Once the farro has cooled, add the green beans, olives, bell pepper, Parmesan, and chives. Stir to combine.

In a small bowl, mix together the sherry vinegar, olive oil, mustard, pepper, and the remaining ½ teaspoon salt. Stir to combine. Pour the sherry vinaigrette over the farro salad. Toss to combine, and serve.

Farro with Coarse Pesto

This is comfort food that's good for you. Farro is an ancient grain that was used to make cereals and pasta before wheat was widely available. It is somewhat similar to Israeli couscous in texture, but if you can't find it, any small pasta shape, such as orzo, makes a good substitute. Don't overwork the pesto; it should still have distinct pieces of the individual herbs, which keeps the flavors clearer and more distinct.

6 to 8 servings

8 cups low-sodium chicken broth
1 pound farro (about 2½ cups)
2 cups fresh flat-leaf parsley leaves
¼ cup fresh basil leaves
2 tablespoons fresh thyme leaves
2 garlic cloves
⅓ cup extra-virgin olive oil
1 tablespoon red wine vinegar
¾ teaspoon salt
½ teaspoon freshly ground black pepper
Wedge of Pecorino Romano cheese,
    for garnish

Bring the chicken broth to a boil in a large saucepan over high heat. Add the farro and stir to combine. Reduce the heat to low, cover the pan, and simmer the farro until tender, about 25 minutes. Drain the farro and set aside in a large bowl.

Meanwhile, in a food processor combine the parsley, basil, thyme, and garlic. Pulse until the herbs are coarsely chopped. Add the olive oil, vinegar, salt, and pepper. Pulse again until the herbs make a coarse mixture.

Toss the warm farro with the coarse pesto. Transfer to a serving bowl. Using a vegetable peeler, make about ½ cup of cheese shavings from the Pecorino cheese wedge. Top the farro with the cheese shavings and serve.

Parmesan Potato Pancake

When I was a personal chef, a family for whom I worked often requested latkes, and though I hadn't made them before, I totally fell in love with them. When I added Parmesan and basil to the mixture, they were even better. The Parmesan melts into a brittle web, like a *frico,* making these extra crisp and delicious.

4 to 6 servings

2 tablespoons olive oil, plus
   1 to 2 tablespoons for frying
1 medium onion, chopped
1 garlic clove, minced
1 teaspoon salt
½ teaspoon freshly ground black pepper
2 pounds Yukon Gold potatoes, peeled
1 cup freshly grated Parmesan cheese
½ cup chopped fresh basil leaves

Warm the 2 tablespoons of olive oil in a large nonstick pan over medium-high heat. Add the onion and cook until translucent, about 4 minutes. Add the garlic and cook until tender and fragrant, about another 2 minutes. Season with salt and pepper. Transfer the onion mixture to a large bowl and set aside.

Meanwhile, grate the potatoes in a food processor using the grating blade. Dump the grated potatoes onto a clean kitchen towel, roll the towel up, and squeeze over the sink to extract as much water from the potatoes as possible. Add the potatoes to the bowl with the onion mixture along with the Parmesan cheese and the basil. Stir to combine and season with additional salt and pepper to taste.

Warm 1 tablespoon of the remaining olive oil over high heat in the same pan you used to cook the onions. When the pan is hot but not smoking, add the potato mixture. Use a spatula to press the mixture down firmly and evenly into the pan. Reduce the heat to medium and cook the pancake until the bottom is golden brown and it can move in the pan, 12 to 15 minutes. Turn the heat down to medium-low if the pancake seems to be browning too fast in places. Slide the pancake onto a large plate, then cover the pancake with a second plate and invert. Turn the heat under the pan back up to high and add a bit more oil if needed. When the pan is hot, slide the pancake back into the skillet, cooking it until the second side is golden and the pancake is cooked through, 12 to 15 minutes longer. Slide the pancake onto a serving platter, cut in wedges, and serve.

Spicy Parmesan
Green Beans and Kale

I always serve this dish at Thanksgiving, but it's good any time during the colder months. The kale and green beans make it vibrant and bright tasting, which is welcome at a time when not many green vegetables are in season.

6 to 8 servings

3 tablespoons olive oil

1 medium onion, sliced

¼ pound cremini mushrooms, trimmed and quartered

1½ pounds green beans, trimmed and cut in 1-inch pieces

2 teaspoons salt

½ teaspoon freshly ground black pepper

¼ cup dry white wine

½ teaspoon red pepper flakes

1 bunch of kale (½ pound), rinsed, stemmed, and coarsely chopped

2 tablespoons freshly squeezed lemon juice

3 tablespoons finely grated Parmesan cheese

Warm the olive oil in a large, heavy sauté pan over medium-high heat. Add the onion and cook, stirring, until translucent, about 4 minutes. Add the mushrooms, green beans, salt, and pepper and cook for 2 minutes. Add the wine and continue cooking until the green beans are almost tender, stirring once or twice, about 5 minutes. Add the red pepper flakes and the kale and continue cooking until the kale has wilted, 4 to 5 minutes. Add the lemon juice and the Parmesan cheese. Toss to coat and serve immediately.

Broiled Zucchini and Potatoes with Parmesan Crust

I know not everyone puts zucchini on their top ten vegetable list, but when you coat zucchini chunks in a delicious Parmesan crust and broil them, trust me, most people will become zucchini lovers. You can cook sweet potatoes or carrots the same way, but zucchini cooks more quickly.

4 servings

4 small new potatoes (red or white, about 1½ inches in diameter)
2 tablespoons unsalted butter
1 garlic clove, minced
1 teaspoon chopped fresh thyme leaves
1 teaspoon chopped fresh rosemary leaves
2 small zucchini, cut in half lengthwise and then in 1-inch pieces
Pinch of kosher salt and freshly ground black pepper
¼ cup freshly grated Parmesan cheese

Bring a medium pot of water to a boil over high heat. Add the potatoes and cook until just tender, 8 to 10 minutes. Drain the potatoes and let cool. When cool, cut the potatoes in half.

Place a medium sauté pan over medium heat. Add the butter, garlic, thyme, and rosemary and heat until the butter melts, about 2 minutes. Meanwhile, season the cut surfaces of the zucchini and potatoes with salt and pepper. Carefully place the zucchini and potatoes cut side down in the melted butter. Cook until golden brown, 12 to 15 minutes.

Preheat the broiler. Line a baking sheet with foil. Place the browned zucchini and potatoes on the baking sheet cut side up. Sprinkle the tops with the Parmesan. Broil until the cheese is golden brown, about 4 minutes. Transfer to a plate and serve.

Artichoke Gratinata

This is the kind of side dish you would find on a steakhouse menu, rich and decadent. Frozen artichokes make this impressive dish quite simple to create. I like to bake it in individual gratin dishes because each serving gets its own crusty browned top, my favorite part!

4 servings

3 tablespoons olive oil
1 garlic clove, minced
1 pound frozen artichoke hearts, thawed
2 tablespoons chopped fresh flat-leaf
    parsley leaves
¾ teaspoon salt
¼ teaspoon freshly ground black pepper
⅛ teaspoon red pepper flakes
½ cup chicken broth
¼ cup Marsala wine
2 tablespoons unsalted butter
⅓ cup plain bread crumbs
⅓ cup freshly grated Parmesan cheese

Preheat the oven to 450°F.

Warm the olive oil in a heavy-bottomed skillet over medium-high heat. Add the garlic and cook for 1 minute. Add the artichoke hearts, parsley, salt, pepper, and red pepper flakes and sauté until the artichoke hearts are starting to brown at the edges, about 3 minutes. Add the chicken broth and wine and simmer for 3 minutes. Transfer the artichoke mixture to a 1½-quart baking dish.

Melt the butter in the same skillet used to cook the artichokes. Add the bread crumbs and stir to coat with the butter. Stir in the Parmesan, then sprinkle the bread-crumb mixture over the artichokes. Bake until the top is golden, about 10 minutes.

Asparagus, Artichoke, and Mushroom Sauté with Tarragon Vinaigrette

Use this recipe as a guideline and a suggestion, as you could really serve any odds and ends you find in the vegetable bin with this versatile vinaigrette. Think about adding broccoli florets, green beans, or summer squash, just to name a few.

4 servings

Tarragon Vinaigrette

- 6 tablespoons extra-virgin olive oil
- 3 tablespoons white wine vinegar
- 2 tablespoons chopped fresh tarragon leaves
- ½ teaspoon salt
- ¼ teaspoon freshly ground black pepper

Vegetable Sauté

- 2 tablespoons olive oil
- 1 large shallot, sliced
- 1 garlic clove, minced
- 8 ounces button mushrooms, trimmed and sliced
- 1 bunch of asparagus (1 pound), trimmed and cut in 3-inch pieces
- 1 (8-ounce) package frozen artichoke hearts, thawed
- ½ pint teardrop tomatoes, halved
- ½ teaspoon salt
- ¼ teaspoon freshly ground black pepper

For the tarragon vinaigrette, combine the oil, vinegar, tarragon, salt, and pepper in a glass screw-top jar. Seal the jar and shake vigorously to mix.

For the vegetable sauté, warm the oil in a large skillet over medium-high heat. Add the shallot and garlic and sauté until tender, about 2 minutes. Add the mushrooms and cook until golden, about 5 minutes, stirring frequently. Add the asparagus and artichokes and cook until the asparagus is tender, about 5 more minutes, stirring occasionally. Turn off the heat and add the tomatoes, salt, and pepper; toss with the vinaigrette.

Transfer to a serving bowl and serve immediately.

Baked Artichokes with Gorgonzola and Herbs

Artichokes take a little time to prepare, but it's time well spent for a dish this extraordinary. The filling becomes hot, bubbly, and creamy, like an individual serving of warm artichoke dip for each diner. You can get most of the prep work out of the way well ahead of time, too; the artichokes can be boiled earlier in the morning and baked later or, if you prefer, the whole dish can be prepared a day in advance, as it reheats very well.

4 servings

4 artichokes

3 lemons

10 ounces mild Gorgonzola cheese, at room temperature

2 tablespoons heavy cream

2 teaspoons chopped fresh thyme leaves

1 tablespoon plus 2 teaspoons chopped fresh flat-leaf parsley leaves

1 garlic clove, finely minced

½ teaspoon salt

½ teaspoon freshly ground black pepper

3 tablespoons plain bread crumbs

1 tablespoon olive oil

Bring a large pot of salted water to a boil over high heat. Trim the artichokes by cutting off the top inch or so. Cut the stem close to the base of the artichoke so the artichoke can stand upright, and remove some of the tough outer leaves. Using kitchen shears, trim the sharp points off of any remaining outer leaves. Drop the artichokes into the boiling water. Halve the lemons and squeeze the juice into the boiling water, then toss in the lemons. Cook the artichokes until tender,

about 30 minutes. Drain the artichokes upside down on a clean kitchen towel and let cool.

Meanwhile, in a small bowl, stir together the Gorgonzola cheese, cream, thyme, 2 teaspoons of the parsley, the garlic, salt, and pepper. In another small bowl, stir together the bread crumbs and the remaining tablespoon of parsley.

Preheat the oven to 400°F. Spread the artichokes open with your fingers and use a small spoon to scrape out the center choke. Stuff the cheese mixture into the artichokes and arrange them in a baking dish. Sprinkle the artichokes with the bread-crumb mixture, then drizzle them with the olive oil. Bake until the artichokes are heated through, the cheese is melted, and the bread crumbs are crisp and golden, about 25 minutes. Transfer the artichokes to a serving dish and serve.

Pasta

WHOLE-WHEAT SPAGHETTI WITH LEMON, BASIL, AND SALMON

PASTINA WITH CLAMS AND MUSSELS

ASPARAGUS LASAGNA

EGGPLANT TIMBALE

TAGLIATELLE WITH SMASHED PEAS, SAUSAGE, AND RICOTTA CHEESE

BAKED ORZO WITH FONTINA AND PEAS

WHOLE-WHEAT LINGUINE WITH GREEN BEANS, RICOTTA, AND LEMON

GIADA'S CARBONARA

PENNE WITH SHRIMP AND HERBED CREAM SAUCE

ORECCHIETTE WITH SAUSAGE, BEANS, AND MASCARPONE

SWISS CHARD AND SWEET PEA MANICOTTI

LEMON RISOTTO

BUTTERNUT SQUASH AND VANILLA RISOTTO

LINGUINE WITH SHRIMP AND LEMON OIL

RIGATONI WITH SQUASH AND PRAWNS

PENNE WITH EGGPLANT PURÉE

RIGATONI WITH VEGETABLE BOLOGNESE

ORZO-STUFFED PEPPERS

PASTA

Next to chocolate, pasta is my favorite food. It's inexpensive, versatile, and appealing in all its various sizes and shapes. Most important, pasta is delicious. It can satisfy a hungry crowd or serve as an intimate dinner for two. It rarely disappoints when it's prepared properly, and it makes a perfect meal, with or without a protein. Serve my Rigatoni with Squash and Prawns on a special occasion; it looks so elegant but tastes like something Grandma could have prepared. Try the Baked Orzo with Fontina and Peas when you're in the mood for something rich and comforting, and be sure to give some of the whole-wheat pasta recipes a try; the flavor and texture of whole-wheat pasta has definitely improved in the past few years. One of my favorite weeknight dinners is Whole-Wheat Linguine with Green Beans, Ricotta, and Lemon. It's quick and easy but it makes me feel good about what I'm eating and fills me up! What more can you ask for from a pasta recipe?

Whole-Wheat Spaghetti with Lemon, Basil, and Salmon

If you're looking for a healthy pasta dish, you can't go wrong with this one. The spinach doesn't really cook, it just gets wilted by the heat of the warm pasta. When I eat this I feel I've both indulged a craving for pasta *and* treated myself to something especially healthful and nutritious!

4 servings

½ pound whole-grain or whole-wheat spaghetti
1 garlic clove, minced
2 tablespoons extra-virgin olive oil
½ teaspoon salt, plus more for seasoning
½ teaspoon freshly ground black pepper, plus more for seasoning
1 tablespoon olive oil
4 (4-ounce) salmon fillets
¼ cup chopped fresh basil leaves
3 tablespoons capers, rinsed and drained
Zest of 1 lemon
2 tablespoons freshly squeezed lemon juice
2 cups fresh baby spinach leaves

Bring a large pot of salted water to a boil over high heat. Add the pasta and cook until tender but still firm to the bite, stirring occasionally, 8 to 10 minutes. Drain the pasta and transfer to a large bowl. Add the garlic, extra-virgin olive oil, salt, and pepper and toss to combine.

Meanwhile, warm the olive oil in a medium skillet over medium-high heat. Season the salmon fillets with salt and pepper. Add the fish to the pan and cook until medium-rare, about 2 minutes per side, depending on the thickness of the fish. Remove the salmon from the pan.

Add the basil, capers, lemon zest, and lemon juice to the spaghetti and toss to combine. Set out 4 serving plates or shallow bowls. Place ½ cup spinach in each bowl. Top with one quarter of the pasta. Top each mound of pasta with a piece of salmon. Serve immediately.

Pastina with Clams and Mussels

Pastina refers to any tiny pasta shape, whether it's stars, little squares, tiny shells, or *riso*. When you boil the pasta, undercook it just a tiny bit so it can cook together with the mussels and the clams for a few minutes, absorbing all that delicious liquid without getting mushy. In that way it's almost like a risotto, but much easier to make.

4 to 6 servings

3 cups low-sodium chicken broth
1 tablespoon kosher salt, plus more for seasoning
1 pound pastina pasta or fregola (see page 81)
¼ cup plus 3 tablespoons olive oil
1 medium onion, chopped
Freshly ground black pepper
2 garlic cloves, chopped
1 cup dry Marsala wine or dry sherry
1 cup (6 ounces) grape tomatoes
12 littleneck clams, scrubbed
12 mussels, scrubbed and debearded
½ cup chopped fresh flat-leaf parsley leaves

In a large pot, combine the chicken broth, 3 cups of water, and 1 tablespoon of salt, and bring to a boil over high heat. Add the pasta and cook until tender but still firm to the bite, stirring occasionally, 5 to 6 minutes. Drain.

While the pasta is cooking, heat ¼ cup of the oil in a large Dutch oven over medium-high heat. Add the onion, season with salt and pepper, and cook until soft, 5 to 7 minutes. Add the garlic and cook for 1 minute longer. Add the Marsala and grape tomatoes and cook for 1 minute, scraping up the brown bits that cling to the bottom of the pan with a wooden spoon. Add the clams and mussels to the pan, cover with a tight-fitting lid, and cook until all the shellfish have opened, 5 to 8 minutes. Discard any shellfish that do not open.

Using tongs, remove the clams and mussels from the pan and reserve. Transfer the pasta to a large serving bowl. Pour the shellfish cooking liquid and vegetables over the pasta, add the remaining 3 tablespoons of olive oil, sprinkle with ¼ cup of the parsley, and toss. Arrange the clams and mussels on top of the pasta and sprinkle with the remaining parsley.

Asparagus Lasagna

If you find regular lasagna with a tomato sauce too heavy for summer meals, this is a great alternative, and it's a real stunner on the plate. A sun-dried tomato pesto is layered between the pasta and vegetables, adding a bit of sweetness to the dish.

6 to 8 servings

1 tablespoon plus 1 teaspoon olive oil
9 lasagna sheets, fresh or dried
2 (8.5-ounce) jars sun-dried tomatoes, drained
1½ cups fresh basil leaves, packed
1¼ cups freshly grated Parmesan cheese
¼ pound pancetta, diced
1 medium onion, diced
2 garlic cloves, minced
4 bunches of asparagus, trimmed and cut into 1-inch pieces
1 (15-ounce) container whole-milk ricotta cheese
1 teaspoon salt
½ teaspoon freshly ground black pepper
2 cups shredded whole-milk mozzarella cheese
2 tablespoons unsalted butter, cut into small pieces

Bring a large pot of salted water to a boil over high heat. Add the teaspoon of olive oil. Add the pasta and cook until tender but still firm to the bite, stirring occasionally, 8 to 10 minutes for dried pasta or 2 to 3 minutes for fresh pasta. Drain the pasta.

In a food processor, combine the sun-dried tomatoes and basil. Pulse until the mixture is combined. Transfer to a small bowl and stir in ½ cup of the Parmesan cheese. Set aside.

In a large skillet, brown the pancetta until crisp. Remove from the pan using a slotted spoon. Add the tablespoon of olive oil, the onion, and garlic to the same skillet and cook until tender, about 4 minutes. Add the asparagus and cook until tender, about 4 minutes, then transfer the mixture to a large bowl. Add the ricotta, salt, and pepper and stir to combine.

Preheat the oven to 350°F. Sprinkle some of the sun-dried tomato mixture over the bottom of a 9 x 13-inch baking dish. Place a layer of lasagna sheets on top of the sun-dried tomato mixture and spread the noodles with half of the asparagus mixture. Sprinkle with a third of the mozzarella cheese and a third of the remaining ¾ cup Parmesan cheese. Make another layer in the same fashion. Top with a third layer of lasagna sheets, some sun-dried tomato mixture, and the remaining mozzarella and Parmesan. Dot the top with the butter. Bake until the lasagna is heated through and the cheese is melted, about 25 minutes.

Eggplant Timbale

When my family and I made trips back to Italy to visit my grandfather's family in Naples, his sisters often made one of these impressive timbales. It looked a bit plain on the outside, but when you cut into it, it was always filled with a delicious mixture, and as a kid I thought it was just *so* cool. I still do.

4 to 6 servings

2 medium eggplants, sliced lengthwise ¼ inch thick
⅓ cup plus 2 tablespoons olive oil
Salt and freshly ground black pepper
½ pound penne pasta
1 medium onion, diced
½ pound lean ground beef
½ pound Italian pork sausage
¼ cup Marsala wine
1 cup frozen peas, thawed
2 cups marinara sauce, jarred or homemade (page 144)
1½ cups diced smoked mozzarella cheese (about 6 ounces)
1 cup freshly grated Pecorino Romano cheese
1 cup chopped fresh basil leaves

Place a grill pan over medium-high heat or preheat a gas or charcoal grill. Using a pastry brush, lightly brush the eggplant slices with ⅓ cup of the olive oil and sprinkle with salt and pepper. Grill the eggplant on both sides until tender and colored with grill marks, about 4 minutes per side. Set aside.

While the eggplant cooks, bring a large pot of salted water to a boil over high heat. Add the pasta and cook until tender but still firm to the bite, stirring occasionally, 8 to 10 minutes. Drain the pasta.

Meanwhile, warm the remaining 2 tablespoons of olive oil in a large skillet over medium-high heat. Add the onion and sauté until tender, about 3 minutes. Add the ground beef and sausage to the pan and brown the meat, breaking it into bite-size pieces with a wooden spoon, about 5 minutes. Pour off any excess fat. Add the Marsala and cook until the liquid has evaporated, about 3 minutes. Turn off the heat. Add the peas and marinara sauce and stir to combine. Add the mozzarella, ¾ cup of the Pecorino, the basil, and the cooked pasta. Season with salt and pepper.

Preheat the oven to 350°F. Line a 9-inch springform pan with the grilled eggplant, making sure that the slices overlap and hang over the edge of the pan; reserve a few slices. Fill the pan with the pasta mixture, pressing down to make sure the filling is evenly distributed. Fold the eggplant slices up over the top of the pasta and top with the reserved slices to enclose the timbale completely. Bake the timbale until the filling is warmed through and the cheese has melted, about 30 minutes. Let the timbale cool for 10 minutes.

Invert the timbale onto a serving plate and remove the pan. Sprinkle with the remaining ¼ cup grated Pecorino, slice, and serve.

Tagliatelle with Smashed Peas, Sausage, and Ricotta Cheese

Todd loves frozen peas and he loves sausage, so this is his kind of recipe, and I created it with him in mind. When you smash the peas, they release their starches into the sauce, making it thick and creamy. To make life a little easier, use a potato masher to smash the peas.

4 to 6 servings

1 pound fresh or dried tagliatelle
   (or other wide, long pasta)
2 tablespoons olive oil
2 garlic cloves, chopped
1 pound hot Italian sausage, casings
   removed
1 pound frozen peas, thawed
1 cup whole-milk ricotta cheese
1 bunch of fresh basil leaves, chopped
   (about ¾ cup)
¼ cup freshly grated Pecorino Romano
   cheese
1 teaspoon salt

Bring a large pot of salted water to a boil over high heat. Add the pasta and cook until tender but still firm to the bite, stirring occasionally, 8 to 10 minutes if dry or according to package directions if fresh. Drain the pasta, reserving 1 cup of the pasta cooking water.

Meanwhile, heat the olive oil and garlic in a large, heavy skillet over medium-high heat until the garlic is fragrant. Add the sausage and cook, using a wooden spoon to break it up into bite-size bits. When the sausage has browned, about 5 minutes, push it over to one side of the pan. Add the peas to the pan and, using the back of the wooden spoon, smash the peas. Turn off the heat. Add the ricotta cheese to the pan and stir to combine, then add the cooked pasta and toss to coat. Add the pasta cooking water ¼ cup at a time, if needed, to make the pasta moist. Add the basil, Pecorino, and salt. Toss gently to combine and serve immediately.

Baked Orzo with Fontina and Peas

In my family, baked pastas were always the crowd-pleasers, and I still love them—especially the crusty, cheesy tops. Full of cream and butter, this is a rich indulgence. Put it together a day ahead of time and bake it just before serving if you like.

6 to 8 servings

4 cups low-sodium chicken broth
1 pound orzo pasta
3 tablespoons unsalted butter, plus more to grease the baking dish
1 onion, chopped
8 ounces white mushrooms, trimmed and sliced
1 cup Marsala wine
½ cup heavy cream
4 ounces shredded fontina cheese (about 1 cup)
4 ounces diced fresh mozzarella cheese (about 1 cup)
1 cup frozen peas, thawed
½ teaspoon salt
½ teaspoon freshly ground black pepper
½ cup plain bread crumbs
¼ cup freshly grated Parmesan cheese
1 teaspoon dried thyme

Preheat the oven to 400°F. Butter a 9 x 13-inch baking dish.

Bring the chicken broth to a boil over medium-high heat in a medium saucepan. Add the orzo and cook until almost tender, about 7 minutes. Pour the orzo and the broth into a large heat-proof bowl. Set aside.

Meanwhile, melt the butter over medium heat in a medium skillet. Add the onion and sauté until tender, about 3 minutes. Add the mushrooms and continue to sauté until the mushrooms are beginning to turn golden around the edges, about 7 minutes. Add the Marsala. Scrape the brown bits off the bottom of the pan and cook until the Marsala has reduced by half, about 5 minutes. Add the mushroom mixture to the orzo in the large bowl, then add the cream, fontina, mozzarella, peas, salt, and pepper. Stir to combine. Pour the mixture into the prepared baking dish.

In a small bowl, combine the bread crumbs, Parmesan, and thyme. Sprinkle the bread-crumb mixture on top of the pasta. Bake until golden on top, about 25 minutes.

Whole-Wheat Linguine with Green Beans, Ricotta, and Lemon

Not all cream sauces are super-rich. This pasta gets its creamy sauce from a combination of part-skim ricotta and pasta water, which come together to make a really easy, lighter cream sauce. Don't leave out the lemon zest; it brightens the flavor and adds a wonderful lemony aroma as well.

4 to 6 servings

1 pound whole-wheat linguine
½ cup part-skim ricotta cheese
3 tablespoons olive oil
½ pound French green beans (haricots verts), trimmed and halved lengthwise
1 garlic clove, chopped
1 teaspoon salt
½ teaspoon freshly ground black pepper
1 cup halved cherry tomatoes
Zest of 1 lemon

Bring a large pot of salted water to a boil over high heat. Add the pasta and cook until tender but still firm to the bite, stirring occasionally, 8 to 10 minutes. Drain the pasta, reserving 1 cup of the cooking water. Transfer the hot pasta to a large heat-proof bowl and add the ricotta. Toss to combine.

Meanwhile, in a large, heavy skillet, warm the olive oil over medium-high heat. Add the green beans, garlic, salt, and pepper and sauté for 4 minutes. Add the reserved pasta cooking liquid and continue cooking until the beans are tender, about 4 more minutes. Add the ricotta-coated pasta to the pan with the green beans and toss to combine. Add the tomatoes and toss gently. Transfer to a serving plate and sprinkle with the lemon zest. Serve.

Giada's Carbonara

My brother and sister and I craved this dish so often as kids that we finally learned to make it ourselves; it is actually one of the first dishes I ever made for myself. These days I consider it special-occasion food, not everyday fare, and it's especially good for Sunday brunch. Add champagne and a fruit salad and you're done. The basil aioli keeps for up to a week in the fridge and it works as a dip for veggies, or as a sandwich spread.

4 to 6 servings

1 bunch of asparagus, ends trimmed, rubber band left on

Basil Aioli
1 garlic clove, minced
2 large egg yolks (see Note)
2 teaspoons Dijon mustard
1 teaspoon freshly squeezed lemon juice
¼ cup finely chopped fresh basil leaves
½ teaspoon salt
¼ teaspoon freshly ground black pepper
⅛ teaspoon cayenne pepper
½ cup vegetable oil
½ cup extra-virgin olive oil

1 pound linguine
1 cup shaved Pecorino Romano cheese (about 4 ounces)
Salt and freshly ground black pepper
4 tablespoons (½ stick) unsalted butter
4 to 6 large eggs

Bring a large pot of salted water to a boil over high heat. Add the asparagus bundle and cook for 3 minutes. Use tongs to transfer the asparagus to a bowl of ice water and let sit until cool, about 5 minutes. Drain the asparagus, remove the rubber band, and cut into 1-inch pieces.

Make the basil aioli: While the asparagus cooks, combine the garlic, egg yolks, mustard, lemon juice, basil, salt, pepper, and cayenne in a food processor and run the machine to mix. With the machine running, slowly drizzle in the vegetable and olive oils.

Meanwhile, add the pasta to the same pot of salted water used to cook the asparagus and cook until tender but still firm to the bite, stirring occasionally, 8 to 10 minutes. Drain the pasta and place in a large bowl. Add 1 cup basil aioli, the asparagus, the shaved cheese, ½ teaspoon salt, and ½ teaspoon pepper and combine. Turn out onto a serving platter.

Melt the butter in a skillet over medium-high heat. Add the eggs, sprinkle with salt and pepper, and fry to your liking. Place the eggs atop the pasta and serve.

Note: This recipe includes raw egg yolks, which are not recommended for children, the elderly, or those with compromised immune systems. If you have health concerns about raw eggs, choose a different recipe.

Penne with Shrimp and Herbed Cream Sauce

This dish is comforting yet elegant, which is why I like to serve it at gatherings during the winter holidays. Best of all, it's a very quick and easy go-to recipe for when you're short on time and need to deliver something special.

4 to 6 servings

1 pound penne pasta
¼ cup olive oil
1 pound medium shrimp, peeled and
    deveined
4 garlic cloves, minced
½ teaspoon kosher salt, plus more
    to taste
½ teaspoon freshly ground black
    pepper, plus more to taste
1 (15-ounce) can whole tomatoes,
    drained and roughly chopped
½ cup chopped fresh basil
½ cup chopped fresh flat-leaf parsley
¼ teaspoon crushed red pepper flakes
1 cup dry white wine
⅓ cup bottled clam juice
¾ cup heavy cream
½ cup grated Parmesan cheese

Bring a large pot of salted water to a boil over high heat. Add the pasta and cook until tender but still firm to the bite, stirring occasionally, 8 to 10 minutes. Drain the pasta and set aside.

In a large skillet, heat the oil over medium-high heat. Add the shrimp, garlic, ½ teaspoon of salt, and ½ teaspoon of pepper. Cook, stirring frequently, until the shrimp turn pink and are cooked through, about 3 minutes. Using a slotted spoon, remove the shrimp from the pan and set aside.

Add the tomatoes, ¼ cup of the basil, ¼ cup of the parsley, and the red pepper flakes to the skillet and cook for 2 minutes, stirring constantly. Add the wine and simmer for another 2 minutes. Add the clam juice and cream. Bring the mixture to a boil. Reduce the heat to medium-low and simmer for 7 to 8 minutes until the sauce thickens.

Add ¼ cup of the Parmesan cheese, the cooked shrimp, the drained pasta, and the remaining basil and parsley. Toss together until all ingredients are coated with the sauce. Season to taste with salt and pepper.

Transfer the pasta to a large serving bowl. Sprinkle with the remaining cheese and serve immediately.

Orecchiette with Sausage, Beans, and Mascarpone

Orecchiete are like little spoons that cup the ingredients and ensure you get a little bit of all the flavors in every bite. This is a particularly fast dish to put together.

4 to 6 servings

1 pound orecchiette or other small shaped pasta
2 tablespoons olive oil
½ pound turkey sausage, casings removed
1 small onion, chopped
1 (15-ounce) can cannellini beans, drained and rinsed
2 tablespoons chopped fresh oregano leaves
½ cup mascarpone cheese
1 teaspoon salt
½ teaspoon freshly ground black pepper

Bring a large pot of salted water to a boil over high heat. Add the pasta and cook until tender but still firm to the bite, stirring occasionally, 8 to 10 minutes. Drain the pasta, reserving 1 cup of the cooking water.

In a large, heavy skillet, warm the olive oil over medium-high heat. Add the sausage and onion and cook, using a wooden spoon to break up the sausage into bite-size pieces as it browns. Continue cooking until the sausage is golden and the onion is tender. Add the beans and oregano and cook for 2 more minutes. Add the reserved pasta cooking water and stir, scraping up any brown bits from the bottom of the pan. Add the mascarpone cheese and stir until it dissolves into a light sauce. Add the salt, pepper, and hot pasta. Stir until coated, and serve.

Swiss Chard and Sweet Pea Manicotti

This dish is real comfort food without the meat. It's great for Sunday family dinners, as a side or a main course, and an equally great way to sneak some greens into your diet. You'll need a pastry bag fitted with a large round tip for this recipe.

12 manicotti (4 to 6 servings)

Butter, for greasing the pan
12 manicotti or cannelloni pasta shells

Filling
1 bunch (about 12 ounces) red or white Swiss chard
2 tablespoons olive oil
1 medium onion, chopped
1 garlic clove, minced
1 (15-ounce) container whole-milk ricotta cheese
¾ cup frozen petite peas, thawed
1 cup (4 ounces) shredded mozzarella cheese
¾ cup (2 ounces) grated Parmesan cheese
¼ cup chopped fresh basil
¾ teaspoon kosher salt
¼ teaspoon freshly ground black pepper

Fontina Fonduta Sauce
¾ cup whole milk
½ cup heavy cream
3 cups (6 ounces) grated fontina cheese
2 tablespoons grated Parmesan cheese
2 tablespoons chopped fresh basil

1½ cups (6 ounces) shredded mozzarella cheese

Preheat the oven to 400°F. Grease a 13 x 9-inch glass baking dish liberally with butter.

Bring a large pot of salted water to a boil over high heat. Add the pasta and cook until tender but still firm to the bite, stirring occasionally, 6 to 8 minutes. Drain the pasta and rinse with cold water. Set aside.

For the filling: Using kitchen scissors or a knife, remove the Swiss chard stems. Chop the leaves into 1-inch pieces. In a large non-stick skillet, heat the olive oil over medium-high heat. Add the onion and cook until soft, 5 to 7 minutes. Add the garlic and cook 1 minute longer, then add the chard and cook, stirring constantly, until wilted, about 2 minutes. Allow the mixture to cool slightly.

recipe continues

Place the ricotta cheese, peas, mozzarella cheese, Parmesan cheese, basil, salt, and pepper in the bowl of a food processor. Add the cooled chard mixture and blend until smooth. Spoon the mixture into the prepared pastry bag and stuff each manicotti shell with the filling. Place the stuffed manicotti in the prepared baking dish.

For the fontina fonduta sauce: In a medium heavy-bottomed saucepan, bring the milk and cream to a simmer over medium heat. Reduce the heat to low. Add the fontina cheese and cook, stirring constantly, until the cheese is melted and the mixture is smooth. Remove the pan from the heat. Stir in the Parmesan cheese and basil.

Pour the sauce over the stuffed manicotti and sprinkle with the 1½ cups mozzarella cheese. Bake for 30 to 35 minutes, until the top is golden. Let the baked manicotti stand for 5 minutes before serving.

Lemon Risotto

Creamy, lemony, and delicious, either as an entrée or a side dish. For a fun, elegant touch, serve individual side-dish portions in a hollowed-out lemon cup (see Note). It would make a pretty, festive accompaniment to almost any springtime meal.

4 entrée servings or 8 side-dish or appetizer servings

4 cups low-sodium chicken broth
½ cup freshly squeezed lemon juice (from 2 to 3 lemons)
3 tablespoons unsalted butter
2 large shallots, diced
1½ cups Arborio rice
½ cup dry white wine
½ cup freshly grated Parmesan cheese, plus 2 tablespoons
¼ cup mascarpone cheese
Zest of ½ lemon
¾ teaspoon kosher salt
¾ teaspoon freshly ground black pepper
2 tablespoons chopped flat-leaf parsley

In a medium saucepan, bring the broth and ¼ cup of lemon juice to a simmer. Cover the broth and keep hot over low heat.

In a medium, heavy saucepan, melt 2 tablespoons of the butter over medium heat. Add the shallots and sauté until tender but not brown, about 3 minutes. Add the rice and stir to coat with the butter. Add the wine and remaining ¼ cup of lemon juice and simmer until it has almost completely evaporated, about 3 minutes. Add ½ cup of the simmering broth and stir until almost completely absorbed, about 2 minutes. Continue cooking the rice, adding the broth ½ cup at a time, stirring constantly and allowing each addition of the broth to absorb before adding the next, until the rice is tender but still firm to the bite and the mixture is creamy, about 20 minutes. Remove from the heat. Stir in the remaining tablespoon of butter, ½ cup of the Parmesan, and the mascarpone cheese, lemon zest, and the salt and pepper. Sprinkle with the remaining 2 tablespoons of Parmesan, garnish with the parsley, and serve.

Note: To serve the risotto in a lemon cup, cut ¼ inch off the bottom of 6 lemons so they stand upright. Slice 1 inch off the stem end. Using a grapefruit spoon, scoop out the flesh of the lemon and discard. Fill each lemon with about ½ cup of risotto. Sprinkle the tops with the remaining 2 tablespoons of grated Parmesan and serve.

Butternut Squash and Vanilla Risotto

I first tasted a risotto similar to this one in South Africa and though at first the idea of adding vanilla to a savory dish sounded a bit odd, I found the flavor combination irresistible. The vanilla adds a lovely aromatic finish but not a lot of sweetness. I consider this the perfect fall dish.

4 entrée servings or 8 side-dish servings

4 cups vegetable broth
1 large vanilla bean
3 cups butternut squash cut in 1-inch squares (about 12 ounces)
3 tablespoons unsalted butter
¾ cup finely chopped onion (from 1 onion)
1½ cups Arborio rice or medium-grain white rice
½ cup dry white wine
½ cup freshly grated Parmesan cheese
½ teaspoon salt
2 tablespoons finely chopped fresh chives

In a medium saucepan, warm the broth over medium-high heat. Cut the vanilla bean in half lengthwise. Scrape out the seeds and add them and the bean to the broth. When the broth comes to a simmer, reduce the heat to low. Add the butternut squash to the simmering broth and cook until tender, about 5 minutes. Use a slotted spoon to transfer the cooked squash to a side dish. Turn the heat on the broth down to very low and cover to keep warm.

Meanwhile, in a large, heavy saucepan, melt 2 tablespoons of the butter over medium heat. Add the onion and sauté until tender but not brown, about 3 minutes. Add the rice and stir to coat with the butter. Add the wine and simmer until the wine has almost completely evaporated, about 3 minutes. Add ½ cup of the simmering broth and stir until almost completely absorbed, about 2 minutes. Continue cooking the rice, adding the broth ½ cup at a time, stirring constantly and allowing each addition of broth to absorb before adding the next, until the rice is tender but still firm to the bite and the mixture is creamy, about 20 minutes total. Discard the vanilla bean.

Turn off the heat under the risotto (and the remaining broth, if any). Gently stir in the butternut squash, Parmesan cheese, the remaining tablespoon of butter, and the salt. Transfer the risotto to a serving bowl and sprinkle with the chives. Serve immediately.

Linguine with Shrimp and Lemon Oil

This variation on my favorite arugula and shrimp salad—served over pasta—tastes as good as it looks. If you keep frozen shrimp in the freezer, a practice I always recommend, this is actually a quick pantry meal, perfect for those late winter/early spring days when everyone wants to start eating a bit lighter.

4 to 6 servings

Lemon Oil
½ cup extra-virgin olive oil
Zest of 1 lemon

Pasta
1 pound linguine
2 tablespoons olive oil
2 shallots, diced
2 garlic cloves, minced
1 pound shrimp, fresh or thawed frozen, peeled and deveined
Zest of 1 lemon
¼ cup freshly squeezed lemon juice (from about 2 lemons)
1 teaspoon salt
½ teaspoon freshly ground black pepper
3 ounces arugula (about 3 packed cups)
¼ cup chopped fresh flat-leaf parsley leaves

To make the lemon oil, combine the olive oil and the lemon zest in a small bowl and set aside.

For the pasta, bring a large pot of salted water to a boil over high heat. Add the pasta and cook until tender but still firm to the bite, stirring occasionally, 8 to 10 minutes. Drain the pasta, reserving 1 cup of the pasta cooking water.

Meanwhile, in a large, heavy skillet, warm the olive oil over medium heat. Add the shallots and garlic and cook for 2 minutes. Add the shrimp and cook until pink, about 5 minutes. Add the cooked linguine, the lemon zest, lemon juice, salt, and pepper. Toss to combine. Turn off the heat and add the arugula. Using a mesh sieve, strain the lemon oil into the pasta; the zest can be discarded. Add the chopped parsley to the pasta and toss to combine. Serve immediately.

Rigatoni with Squash and Prawns

This recipe comes from a beachside cafe in Capri. Prawns are very popular in Europe, where they are abundant, but here they are a bit harder to find and a little more expensive. Feel free to substitute extra-large shrimp in their place—or leave them out altogether. It will still be a very satisfying, hearty meal. The squash makes the most luxurious, velvety sauce imaginable, with a beautiful orange color.

4 to 6 servings

6 tablespoons olive oil

1 pound butternut squash, peeled and cut into 1-inch cubes

2 garlic cloves, minced

2 teaspoons salt

¾ teaspoon freshly ground black pepper

1 cup vegetable broth

1 pound rigatoni pasta

1 pound prawns or large shrimp, peeled and deveined

¾ to 1 cup whole milk

½ cup chopped fresh basil leaves

¼ cup freshly grated Parmesan cheese

Warm 3 tablespoons of the olive oil in a large, heavy skillet over medium-high heat. Add the butternut squash, garlic, 1 teaspoon of the salt, and ¼ teaspoon of the pepper. Sauté until the squash is golden and tender, 5 to 7 minutes. Add the vegetable broth, bring to a simmer, cover, and cook until the squash is very soft, another 5 to 7 minutes.

Transfer the squash mixture to a blender or food processor and purée.

Bring a large pot of salted water to a boil over high heat. Add the pasta and cook until tender but still firm to the bite, stirring occasionally, 8 to 10 minutes. Drain the pasta.

Meanwhile, warm the remaining 3 tablespoons of olive oil in a large, heavy skillet over medium-high heat. Sprinkle the prawns with the remaining 1 teaspoon of salt and remaining ½ teaspoon of pepper. Add the prawns to the pan and cook, turning once, until just pink, about 3 minutes.

In a large pot over low heat, combine the cooked pasta, puréed squash mixture, and ¾ cup milk. Stir to combine. Add the remaining ¼ cup milk if the sauce needs to be moistened. Add the cooked prawns, the basil, and the cheese. Stir until warm and serve.

Penne with Eggplant Purée

Roasting brings out the best flavors in fall vegetables, and it's a super-easy way to cook them, as well: just cut them into cubes and let the oven do the rest. Once puréed they become a warm, mellow sauce that collects in the tubular pasta, so that when you bite one the flavors explode in your mouth.

4 to 6 servings

1 medium eggplant, unpeeled, cut into 1-inch cubes
1 pint cherry tomatoes
3 garlic cloves, whole
3 tablespoons olive oil
1 teaspoon salt
1 teaspoon freshly ground black pepper
1 teaspoon red pepper flakes
¼ cup pine nuts
1 pound penne pasta
¼ cup torn fresh mint leaves
3 tablespoons extra-virgin olive oil
½ cup freshly grated Parmesan cheese

Preheat the oven to 400°F. Line a baking sheet with parchment paper.

In a large bowl, combine the eggplant, cherry tomatoes, garlic, olive oil, salt, pepper, and red pepper flakes. Spread the vegetables on the prepared baking sheet in an even layer. Roast in the oven until the vegetables are tender and the eggplant is golden, about 35 minutes.

While the vegetables are roasting, place the pine nuts in a small baking dish. Place in the oven on the rack below the vegetables. Roast until golden, about 8 minutes, stirring once. Remove from the oven and transfer to a bowl to cool.

Meanwhile, bring a large pot of salted water to a boil over high heat. Add the pasta and cook until tender but still firm to the bite, stirring occasionally, 8 to 10 minutes. Drain the pasta, reserving 1½ cups of the cooking liquid, and transfer the pasta to a large bowl.

Transfer the roasted vegetables to a food processor. Add the torn mint leaves and the extra-virgin olive oil. Pulse until the vegetables are puréed, but don't make it too smooth; it should be a bit chunky with some distinct bits of vegetables.

Transfer the puréed vegetables to the bowl with the pasta. Add the Parmesan cheese. Stir to combine, adding the pasta cooking liquid ½ cup at a time until the pasta is saucy. Sprinkle the pine nuts over the top and serve.

Rigatoni with Vegetable Bolognese

I've made this a *lot*. Even though it's completely vegetarian, it tastes very full-bodied and complex, with a deep, winy flavor that even meat-lovers will enjoy. I serve it often when I am cooking for a crowd and don't know how many vegetarians may be in the group.

6 to 8 servings

1 ounce dried porcini mushrooms
1½ cups very hot water
3 carrots, peeled and chopped
1 onion, peeled and chopped
1 red bell pepper, cored, seeded, and chopped
2 garlic cloves
¼ cup olive oil
2 teaspoons chopped fresh thyme leaves
1 teaspoon chopped fresh oregano leaves
2 teaspoons salt
1 teaspoon freshly ground black pepper
5 ounces assorted mushrooms (such as shiitake, cremini, and brown), stemmed and chopped
2 tablespoons tomato paste
½ cup red wine
½ cup mascarpone cheese
1 pound rigatoni pasta
¼ cup freshly grated Parmesan cheese

Place the dried porcini mushrooms in a small bowl and cover with the hot water. Set aside and let the mushrooms soften.

Place the carrots, onion, bell pepper, and garlic in a food processor. Pulse the vegetables until finely chopped but still chunky. Heat the olive oil in a large, heavy skillet. Add the chopped vegetables, thyme, oregano, salt, and pepper and cook over medium-high heat until tender, about 6 minutes.

Strain the porcini mushrooms, reserving the soaking liquid. Add the porcini mushrooms, fresh mushrooms, and tomato paste and continue cooking, stirring to dissolve the tomato paste, until the mushrooms are softened, about 5 minutes. Add the mushroom soaking liquid and the red wine. Bring the liquid to a boil, reduce the heat to low, and let the mixture simmer until the liquid is reduced by half, about 10 minutes. Add the mascarpone cheese and stir just until the cheese is incorporated.

Meanwhile, bring a large pot of salted water to a boil over high heat. Add the pasta and cook until tender but still firm to the bite, stirring occasionally, 8 to 10 minutes. Drain the pasta, reserving ½ cup of the cooking liquid, and add to the vegetable mixture. Add some of the reserved pasta cooking liquid, if necessary, to moisten the sauce. Toss with the Parmesan and serve.

Orzo-Stuffed Peppers

I love to prepare and serve stuffed peppers because they
make such a beautiful presentation; when you cut into them
and the delicious filling spills out, it's like getting a present.
My mother is also partial to stuffed peppers, which she fills
with vegetables, meat, pasta—almost anything.

4 to 6 servings

1 (28-ounce) can whole Italian tomatoes
2 medium zucchini, grated
½ cup chopped fresh mint leaves
½ cup freshly grated Pecorino Romano
    cheese, plus more for sprinkling
¼ cup extra-virgin olive oil
3 garlic cloves, minced
1 teaspoon salt
1 teaspoon freshly ground black pepper
4 cups low-sodium chicken broth
1½ cups orzo (rice-shaped pasta)
6 sweet bell peppers (red or yellow)
¼ cup chopped fresh basil, for garnish

Preheat the oven to 400°F.

Pour the tomatoes and their juices into a large
bowl and break them into pieces using a pair
of kitchen shears or your fingertips. Add the
zucchini, mint, cheese, olive oil, garlic, salt,
and pepper. Stir to combine.

Meanwhile, bring the chicken broth to a boil
in a medium saucepan over high heat. Add
the orzo and cook for 4 minutes. The orzo will
be only partially cooked. Drain the orzo
through a sieve, reserving the chicken broth,
and add the orzo to the large bowl with the
vegetables. Stir to combine. Transfer the warm
chicken broth to a 3-quart baking dish.

Slice the tops off the peppers and remove all
ribs and seeds. Cut a very thin slice from the
base to help the peppers stand up.

Spoon the orzo mixture into the peppers.
Place the peppers in the baking dish with the
warm chicken broth. Cover the dish with foil
and bake for 45 minutes. Remove the foil,
sprinkle each pepper with cheese, and
continue baking until the cheese is golden,
about 15 minutes. Remove from the oven and
carefully transfer the stuffed peppers to serving plates. Garnish with basil, if desired.

Meat,
Poultry, and Fish

BEEF AND BUTTERNUT SQUASH STEW
RIB-EYE STEAK WITH BLACK OLIVE VINAIGRETTE
BEEF ROAST WITH SPICY PARSLEY TOMATO SAUCE
PROSCIUTTO LAMB BURGERS
LAMB RAGÙ WITH MINT
TURKEY OSSO BUCO WITH PARSLEY AND ROSEMARY GREMOLATA
HERBED CHICKEN WITH SPRING VEGETABLES
CHICKEN WITH BALSAMIC BARBECUE SAUCE
CHICKEN SCALOPPINE WITH SAFFRON CREAM SAUCE
VEAL CHOP SALTIMBOCCA
PORK CHOPS WITH FENNEL AND CAPER SAUCE
PORK CHOPS WITH SWEET ONION MARMELLATA
ROASTED PORK LOIN WITH ROASTED GARLIC VINAIGRETTE
SWORDFISH POACHED IN OLIVE OIL WITH BROCCOLI RABE PESTO
GRILLED SHRIMP IN ARTICHOKE TOMATO BROTH
SALMON WITH PUFF PASTRY AND PESTO
ROASTED HALIBUT WITH GRAPEFRUIT FENNEL SALSA
SALMON IN LEMON BRODETTO WITH PEA PURÉE

MEAT,
POULTRY, AND FISH

Most people don't consider a meal a meal unless it includes some sort of fish, poultry, or meat. What's most important for our diets, though, is that we eat a variety of foods, both proteins and other types. My solution is to serve some of them at every meal, eating small portions of each so that I never have to feel like I'm missing out—or getting weighed down.

Like most people, I include chicken, turkey, and fish as staples, and I'm often asked how to change up those poultry and fish recipes to keep weeknight meals exciting without adding to the stress of the day. You'll find plenty of great options here, from the easy braised Turkey Osso Buco, redolent with aromatics and wine, to a more decadent dish like Chicken Scaloppine with Saffron Cream Sauce. Fish and shrimp get makeovers, too, with lots of veggies and accents, such as fennel and grapefruit salsa for a grilled halibut fillet. And never fear that I have forgotten the meat-lovers. Beef and Butternut Squash Stew and Lamb Ragù with Mint will make you want to curl up on the couch with a glass of wine and hunker down to a cozy dinner.

Beef and Butternut Squash Stew

I'm really in love with butternut squash these days and I have been finding lots of new ways to use it. Here it brightens up beef stew, which can be a bit dreary looking, turning a tired old standard into something more unexpected and elegant.

4 to 6 servings

3 tablespoons olive oil
1 onion, chopped
2 garlic cloves, chopped
1 tablespoon minced fresh rosemary leaves
1 tablespoon chopped fresh thyme leaves
½ teaspoon salt, plus more to taste
½ teaspoon freshly ground black pepper, plus more to taste
2 tablespoons all-purpose flour
2 pounds stew beef, cut into 2-inch cubes
1 cup Marsala wine
1 pound butternut squash, trimmed and cut into 2-inch cubes
¼ cup chopped sun-dried tomatoes
3 to 4 cups beef broth
2 tablespoons chopped fresh flat-leaf parsley leaves
Crusty bread, for serving

In a large soup pot, heat the olive oil over medium heat. Add the onion, garlic, rosemary, and thyme and sauté until the onion is tender, about 4 minutes. Combine the salt, pepper, and flour in a medium bowl. Add the beef cubes and toss to coat with the seasoned flour. Turn up the heat under the soup pot to medium-high and add the beef. Cook until the beef cubes are browned and golden around the edges, about 5 minutes. Add the Marsala and use a wooden spoon to gently stir up all the brown bits off the bottom of the pan. Add the butternut squash and sun-dried tomatoes and stir to combine. Add enough beef broth to just cover the beef and squash. Bring the stew to a boil over high heat, then reduce the heat to low, cover, and simmer for 1 hour. Season the stew with additional salt and pepper to taste. Sprinkle with the chopped parsley. Serve with crusty bread alongside.

Rib-Eye Steak with Black Olive Vinaigrette

Like a lot of men, my husband thinks entertaining begins and ends with grilled steaks, so I'm always looking for different ways to jazz them up and keep it interesting. This bold vinaigrette fits the bill and really stands up to the strong flavor of beef. Make the vinaigrette in advance, throw some steaks on the grill, and you have a great dinner; if you have a veggie friend, you can serve the same versatile vinaigrette over warm pasta.

4 servings

2 (1½-inch-thick) boneless
   rib-eye steaks
1 tablespoon olive oil
1 tablespoon herbes de Provence
1 teaspoon salt
1 teaspoon freshly ground black pepper

Vinaigrette
½ cup black olives, pitted
3 tablespoons red wine vinegar
2 teaspoons Dijon mustard
1 garlic clove
½ teaspoon salt
½ teaspoon freshly ground black pepper
6 tablespoons extra-virgin olive oil
6 tablespoons vegetable oil
2 tablespoons chopped fresh flat-leaf
   parsley leaves

Preheat an outdoor grill or grill pan over medium-high heat. Coat the beef with the olive oil and sprinkle with the herbes de Provence, salt, and pepper. Grill for 6 to 8 minutes per side, or until the meat is medium-rare. Transfer the meat to a cutting board to rest before slicing, tenting it with foil to keep it warm.

To make the black olive vinaigrette, combine the olives, red wine vinegar, mustard, garlic, salt, and pepper in a blender and blend until mixed. In a small pitcher combine the olive oil and vegetable oil. Drizzle the oil into the blender with the machine running. Transfer the vinaigrette to a serving dish. Stir in the parsley.

To serve, cut the steaks in 1-inch-thick slices and serve with the vinaigrette.

Beef Roast with
Spicy Parsley Tomato Sauce

When you roast tomatoes along with beef it gives the dish a slightly acidic edge that cuts the rich, unctuous quality of the meat. The softened tomatoes go straight into the food processor with some vinegar and parsley for a sauce that is both lighter and tangier than the typical brown gravy. Serve with buttered egg noodles.

4 to 6 servings

1 (2- to 2½-pound) sirloin tip or chuck roast
Kosher salt and freshly ground black pepper
4 Roma tomatoes, halved lengthwise
2 teaspoons herbes de Provence
3 tablespoons olive oil
1½ cups fresh flat-leaf parsley leaves
2 garlic cloves
½ teaspoon red pepper flakes
2 tablespoons red wine vinegar
½ cup extra-virgin olive oil

Preheat the oven to 375°F.

Season the beef with salt and pepper. Season the tomatoes with salt, pepper, and herbes de Provence.

Heat the olive oil in a medium, heavy roasting pan or Dutch oven over high heat. Sear the beef on all sides until browned. Place the seasoned tomatoes around the seared beef and place the pan in the oven. Roast until a meat thermometer inserted in the beef reads 130°F for medium-rare or 135°F for medium, 30 to 40 minutes. Tent the roast loosely with foil and let it rest for 10 to 15 minutes. The internal temperature of the meat should rise 5 degrees more and the juices will redistribute into the roast.

While the meat rests, place the parsley and garlic in a food processor and pulse until the parsley is finely chopped. Add the red pepper flakes, ¾ teaspoon salt, the red wine vinegar, and the roasted tomatoes and process until puréed. With the machine running, add the extra-virgin olive oil in a steady stream.

To serve, slice the roast and arrange on a serving platter. Drizzle a little sauce over the meat. Serve the remaining sauce in a small bowl alongside.

Prosciutto Lamb Burgers

If you've cut back on burgers because you don't want to eat the bun, here's your solution. These well-seasoned patties get wrapped in a piece of prosciutto, making them extra juicy. Use your hands to combine the meat mixture; you are less likely to overmix this way.

4 to 6 servings

½ cup plain dried bread crumbs
¼ cup chopped fresh flat-leaf parsley leaves
1 large egg, lightly beaten
2 tablespoons whole milk
½ cup freshly grated Pecorino Romano cheese
¼ cup chopped sun-dried tomatoes
¾ teaspoon salt
¾ teaspoon freshly ground black pepper
1 pound ground lamb
6 large slices prosciutto, sliced medium thin
¼ cup olive oil
Fresh basil leaves, for topping each burger
Fresh tomato slices, for topping each burger
Extra-virgin olive oil, for drizzling
Balsamic vinegar, for drizzling

In a large bowl, combine the bread crumbs, parsley, egg, milk, cheese, sun-dried tomatoes, salt, and pepper. Stir to combine. Add the lamb and work with your fingers until incorporated. Divide the mixture into 6 portions and pat each portion into an inch-thick burger. Place the prosciutto slices on a cutting board or piece of parchment paper. Place 1 lamb burger in the center of each slice of prosciutto and wrap the prosciutto around the burger.

Place a large, heavy skillet over medium heat. Add the olive oil and heat for 2 minutes. Place the lamb burgers in the pan, prosciutto-covered side down, and cook over medium heat until the prosciutto is golden, 6 to 8 minutes. Turn the burgers and finish cooking, 6 to 8 minutes more.

Remove the burgers from the pan and place on a serving platter or individual plates. Top each burger with 2 or 3 basil leaves, 1 or 2 slices of tomato, and a drizzle of extra-virgin olive oil and balsamic vinegar. Serve immediately.

Lamb Ragù with Mint

Ground lamb is now very widely available, and it makes a nice change from the usual beef ragù once in a while. This is thick enough to serve in shallow bowls over rice or simply with some nice bread, but you could also increase the amount of marinara sauce to four cups and serve it over pasta.

4 to 6 servings

2 tablespoons olive oil
2 shallots, chopped
1 garlic clove, minced
1½ pounds ground lamb
½ teaspoon salt
¼ teaspoon freshly ground black pepper
1 cup red wine
2 cups Marinara Sauce (recipe follows, or jarred)
½ cup torn fresh mint leaves
½ cup ricotta cheese

Warm the olive oil in a large skillet over high heat. Add the shallots and garlic and cook until tender, about 3 minutes. Add the ground lamb, salt, and pepper. Cook, stirring and breaking up the meat with a wooden spoon, until the lamb has browned and the juices have evaporated.

Add the wine, scraping up any brown bits from the bottom of the pan. Simmer until the wine has reduced by half. Add the marinara sauce and simmer over low heat until the flavors have blended, about 10 minutes.

Add the mint and ricotta and stir until mixed. Serve in shallow bowls.

Marinara Sauce

Makes about 2 quarts

½ cup extra-virgin olive oil
2 small onions, finely chopped
2 garlic cloves, finely chopped
2 celery stalks, finely chopped
2 carrots, peeled and finely chopped
½ teaspoon sea salt
½ teaspoon freshly ground black pepper
2 (32-ounce) cans crushed tomatoes
2 dried bay leaves

In a large pot, heat the olive oil over medium-high heat. Add the onions and garlic and sauté until the onions are translucent, about 10 minutes. Add the celery, carrots, and salt and pepper. Sauté until all the vegetables are soft, about 10 minutes. Add the tomatoes and bay leaves, and simmer uncovered over low heat until the sauce thickens, about 1 hour. Remove and discard the bay leaves. Season the sauce with more salt and pepper to taste.

Turkey Osso Buco

Here's an osso buco everyone will love. Consider this a nontraditional Thanksgiving meal; you'll get both dark and light meat without having to cook a whole turkey. Using a gremolata to spark up the flavor of a long-cooked dish like this one is a very traditional Italian touch that makes a huge difference in the finished dish.

6 to 8 servings

1 half-breast of turkey, cut into 4 pieces
2 turkey thighs
Salt and freshly ground black pepper
⅓ cup all-purpose flour, for dredging
½ cup vegetable oil
1 small onion, finely diced
1 carrot, peeled and finely diced
1 celery stalk, finely diced
1 tablespoon tomato paste
1 cup dry white wine
4 cups low-sodium chicken broth
1 large fresh rosemary sprig
2 large fresh thyme sprigs
2 bay leaves
2 whole cloves

Gremolata

¼ cup chopped fresh flat-leaf parsley
Zest of 1 lemon
2 garlic cloves, minced
1 teaspoon minced fresh rosemary
Pinch of salt
Pinch of freshly ground black pepper

Preheat the oven to 375°F. Pat the turkey pieces dry with paper towels to ensure even browning. Season the turkey with salt and pepper, then dredge the pieces in the flour, shaking off any excess.

In a heavy roasting pan large enough to fit the turkey pieces in a single layer, heat the oil over medium heat. Add the turkey and cook until browned on both sides, about 6 minutes per side. Transfer to a plate and reserve.

To the same pan, add the onion, carrot, and celery. Season the vegetables with salt and cook until they are tender, about 6 minutes. Stir in the tomato paste and cook for 1 minute. Stir in the wine and simmer until the liquid is reduced by half, about 3 minutes. Return the turkey to the pan. Add enough chicken broth to come two thirds up the sides of the turkey pieces. Add the herb sprigs, bay leaves, and cloves to the pan. Bring the liquid to a boil, then cover the pan tightly with foil and transfer to the oven. Braise until the turkey is fork-tender, about 1 hour and 45 minutes, turning the pieces after 1 hour.

When the turkey is almost done, combine the gremolata ingredients in a bowl. Slice the turkey and arrange it in shallow serving bowls. Season the sauce to taste with salt and pepper and ladle some over each serving. Sprinkle each serving with a large pinch of gremolata.

Herbed Chicken with Spring Vegetables

Intimidated by roasting and carving a whole chicken? This dish is just as aromatic and comforting, but is a lot easier to handle and serve. Everything cooks together in one pan, including the sauce.

4 to 6 servings

¼ cup chopped fresh thyme leaves
¼ cup chopped fresh flat-leaf parsley leaves
3 garlic cloves, minced
1 teaspoon fennel seeds
¼ teaspoon red pepper flakes
Kosher salt
Freshly ground black pepper
3 chicken breast halves, boneless but with the skin
3 chicken thighs
3 tablespoons olive oil
1 tablespoon unsalted butter
6 cipolline onions, trimmed and peeled
8 ounces baby carrots, peeled and trimmed, but leaving on a bit of green tip
1 cup low-sodium chicken broth
6 ounces sugar snap peas, trimmed
4 ounces morel mushrooms

Preheat the oven to 375°F. In a small bowl, combine the thyme, parsley, garlic, fennel seeds, red pepper flakes, and a pinch of salt and pepper. Stir to combine. Place the chicken pieces on a work surface. Gently loosen the skin of the chicken and push the herb mixture under the skin. Season the chicken all over with salt and pepper.

Warm the olive oil in a large skillet over medium-high heat. When the oil is hot, place the chicken in the pan, skin side down. Cook until the skin is crispy and golden, about 5 minutes. Turn the chicken and cook the same way on the other side. Turn off the heat and transfer the chicken to a baking dish, skin side up again. Bake the chicken for about 15 minutes, or until cooked through.

Meanwhile, return the same skillet the chicken was browned in to the stovetop. Add the butter and melt over medium heat. Add the cipolline onions and carrots, sprinkle with salt and pepper, and cook until tender and golden in places, about 7 minutes. Add the chicken broth and scrape any brown bits off the bottom of the pan with a wooden spoon. Add the snap peas and mushrooms. Simmer over low heat until the vegetables are tender and the liquid has reduced by half, about 5 minutes. Taste the sauce and add more salt and pepper if necessary.

Arrange the chicken pieces on a serving platter and spoon the vegetables around them. Spoon the sauce over the chicken. Serve immediately.

Chicken with
Balsamic Barbecue Sauce

Tangy and *sweet* are the best words to describe this barbecue sauce. Make a double batch, take some to your next picnic, and you will thank me.

4 servings

Barbecue Sauce
  1 cup balsamic vinegar
  ¾ cup ketchup
  ⅓ cup brown sugar
  1 garlic clove, minced
  1 tablespoon Worcestershire sauce
  1 tablespoon Dijon mustard
  ½ teaspoon salt
  ½ teaspoon freshly ground black pepper

  1 chicken, cut in serving pieces
    (2 breasts, 2 thighs, 2 legs, and
    2 wings)
  Salt and freshly ground black pepper

Combine all the barbecue sauce ingredients in a small nonreactive saucepan and whisk until the mixture is smooth. Simmer over medium heat until reduced by one third, 15 to 20 minutes.

Place a grill pan over medium heat or preheat an outdoor grill. Season the chicken pieces with salt and pepper.

Transfer ½ cup of the sauce to a small bowl. Grill the chicken for about 10 minutes per side, brushing the chicken with the ½ cup barbecue sauce for the last 2 or 3 minutes. Transfer the chicken to a serving platter and let it rest for at least 5 minutes. Serve with the remaining barbecue sauce alongside.

Note: If you prefer not to grill, the chicken can also be baked. Place the chicken skin side up in a baking dish and bake for 25 minutes in a 375°F oven. Remove the baking dish from the oven and spoon the barbecue sauce all over the top of the chicken. Return the baking dish to the oven and bake for another 15 minutes.

Chicken Scaloppine with Saffron Cream Sauce

What cooks more quickly than thin chicken cutlets? No wonder they are a weeknight mainstay in most homes. With the addition of saffron, though, they become elegant enough to serve to company. Saffron is a pricy ingredient but it adds a beautiful color; and if you store it in a tightly sealed container it will keep for a long time.

4 to 6 servings

2 tablespoons olive oil

1 pound thin chicken cutlets (scaloppine)

¾ teaspoon salt, plus more for seasoning meat

¼ teaspoon freshly ground black pepper, plus more for seasoning meat

2 shallots, sliced

1 garlic clove, minced

½ cup dry white wine

1½ cups low-sodium chicken broth

¼ teaspoon saffron threads

½ cup heavy cream

3 tablespoons chopped fresh flat-leaf parsley leaves (optional)

Warm the olive oil in a large skillet over high heat. Season the chicken cutlets with salt and pepper. Cook the chicken until golden and cooked through, 2 to 3 minutes per side. Transfer the chicken to a serving plate and tent with foil to keep warm.

Reduce the heat to medium, add the shallots and garlic, and cook until tender, about 2 minutes. Deglaze the pan with the white wine, using a wooden spoon to scrape all the brown bits from the bottom of the pan. Cook until the wine is almost evaporated. Add the chicken broth and saffron threads, bring to a simmer, and cook for 10 minutes, or until reduced by half. Add the cream, salt, and pepper to the skillet and stir to combine.

Simmer for 1 minute to blend the flavors. Pour the sauce over the chicken. Sprinkle with the parsley if desired and serve immediately.

Veal Chop Saltimbocca

Traditionally saltimbocca is made with veal cutlets, rather than chops, but a thicker cut of meat makes for a heartier dish. When you sauté the chops the prosciutto forms a great, salty crust on the outside and the lemon gets caramelized, making a yummy, savory package.

4 servings

4 boneless veal loin chops, each about ¾ inch thick
½ teaspoon salt, plus more for seasoning meat
¼ teaspoon freshly ground black pepper, plus more for seasoning meat
4 thin lemon slices
4 sage leaves, plus 1 teaspoon finely chopped fresh sage
4 large slices prosciutto
3 tablespoons olive oil
½ cup dry white wine
½ cup low-sodium chicken broth
1 (14.5-ounce) can whole tomatoes, drained and chopped
½ cup heavy cream

Place the veal chops on a work surface and season with salt and pepper. Place a slice of lemon on top of each chop. Top with one sage leaf. Lay a piece of prosciutto on each chop and press to seal.

Warm the olive oil in a large skillet over medium-high heat. Place the veal chops in the hot oil, lemon-side up, and cook for 6 minutes. Turn the chops over and cook until the prosciutto starts to caramelize, 2 to 3 minutes. Remove from the skillet and tent with foil to keep warm.

Add the white wine to the skillet and deglaze over high heat, scraping up the brown bits from the bottom of the pan with a wooden spoon. Add the chicken broth and reduce by half, about 5 minutes. Add the tomatoes, cream, ½ teaspoon of salt, and ¼ teaspoon of pepper. Stir until combined and hot. Pour some of the sauce over each veal chop and top with the remaining teaspoon of finely chopped sage. Serve immediately.

Pork Chops with Fennel and Caper Sauce

Once primarily available at farmers' markets and gourmet groceries, fennel is available in most supermarkets these days (depending on where you live it might be labeled anise). Its mild licorice flavor has a special affinity for pork and for chicken. This dish is very light and clean, with no thickeners or cream to mute the flavors.

4 servings

¼ cup olive oil

4 (2-inch-thick) boneless pork chops (about 2 pounds total)

¾ teaspoon salt, plus more for seasoning meat

¾ teaspoon freshly ground black pepper, plus more for seasoning meat

2 small fennel bulbs, stalks and fronds removed, thinly sliced crosswise (about 2 cups)

2 large shallots, thinly sliced

⅔ cup chopped fresh flat-leaf parsley leaves

½ cup dry white wine

1 (28-ounce) can diced tomatoes, with their juices

½ lemon, zested

2 tablespoons drained capers

Heat the olive oil in a large, heavy skillet over high heat. Season the pork chops with salt and pepper and brown for about 4 minutes per side. Remove the pork from the pan, cover loosely with foil, and set aside.

Add the fennel, shallots, and ⅓ cup of the chopped parsley to the same skillet and cook over medium heat until the fennel is beginning to brown, about 5 minutes. Add the wine. Using a wooden spoon, scrape the brown bits off the bottom of the pan. Stir in the tomatoes, then return the pork to the pan, nestling the chops among the fennel and tomatoes so they are mostly submerged in the pan juices. Cook until the fennel is tender and the pork is done, 12 to 15 minutes.

Transfer the pork to a serving dish. To finish the sauce, add the lemon zest, the remaining ⅓ cup of chopped parsley, the capers, and ¾ teaspoon each of salt and pepper. Stir to combine. Spoon over the pork chops and serve immediately.

Pork Chops with Sweet Onion Marmellata

Pork is a very popular meat in Italy, but it is eaten more often in the form of sausage or cured. It wasn't until I started to work as a private chef that I realized what a fixture pork chops are on American tables. This is my Italian take on an American classic, pork chops and applesauce; the onions cook down to a jam-like condiment.

4 to 6 servings

Onion Marmellata

- ¼ cup olive oil
- 4 large onions, thinly sliced
- ¼ cup orange marmalade
- 1 tablespoon chopped fresh rosemary
- 1 tablespoon chopped fresh thyme
- 1 teaspoon kosher salt
- 1 teaspoon freshly ground black pepper
- 2 tablespoons balsamic vinegar
- 1 tablespoon sugar (or more to taste)

Pork Chops

- 1 tablespoon chopped fresh rosemary leaves
- 1 tablespoon chopped fresh thyme leaves
- 2 garlic cloves, minced
- 1 teaspoon kosher salt
- 1 teaspoon freshly ground black pepper
- 4 to 6 boneless, center-cut pork chops
- ¼ cup chopped fresh flat-leaf parsley leaves

To make the onion marmellata, place a large, heavy pot over medium-high heat. Add the olive oil and the onions. Stir to combine and cook until starting to sizzle, about 2 minutes, then add the remaining marmellata ingredients. Reduce the heat to low. Cover the pot and cook over low heat for 2 hours, stirring every 30 minutes to scrape up any brown bits. The onions should have a soft, jam-like consistency and a deep mahogany color.

Once the marmellata is simmering, season the pork chops: Combine the rosemary, thyme, garlic, salt, and pepper in a small bowl. Using your fingers, work all the ingredients together until well combined. Rub the herb mixture over the pork chops. Cover with plastic wrap and refrigerate for at least 90 minutes.

About 20 minutes before the onions are finished, remove the pork chops from the refrigerator. Place a grill pan over medium-high heat or preheat a gas or charcoal grill. When hot, grill the pork chops to medium, about 7 minutes per side depending on their thickness or 9 to 10 minutes for well done. To serve, spoon the onion marmellata over the pork chops. Sprinkle with the chopped parsley. Serve immediately.

Roasted Pork Loin with Roasted Garlic Vinaigrette

Few things are easier to make for a group than a roasted pork loin, but sometimes it can be a little bland. Gilding the sliced meat with a bit of mellow, garlicky sauce ensures your Sunday roast will have plenty of flavor and adds moistness as well.

6 to 8 servings

Roasted Garlic
2 heads of garlic
2 tablespoons olive oil
Salt

Pork Loin
1 (3½- to 4½-pound) boneless pork loin
Salt and freshly ground black pepper

Vinaigrette
Roasted garlic (above)
¼ cup chopped fresh flat-leaf parsley leaves
½ cup balsamic vinegar
¾ cup extra-virgin olive oil
1 teaspoon sugar
1 teaspoon salt
½ teaspoon freshly ground black pepper

Preheat the oven to 475°F.

To make the roasted garlic, cut the heads of garlic in half crosswise. Place the garlic halves on a sheet of foil, drizzle them with the olive oil, and sprinkle with salt. Fold the foil up and around the garlic halves, making sure they stay upright. Seal the foil into an airtight package. Roast until the garlic cloves are golden and soft, about 60 minutes. Keep the garlic in the foil and cool slightly.

Thirty minutes after the garlic has started roasting, place the pork loin in a medium, heavy roasting pan. Season on all sides with salt and pepper. Roast the pork along with the garlic until an instant-read thermometer registers 140 to 145°F, 30 to 40 minutes. Remove the roasting pan from the oven, tent the pork with foil, and let rest for 15 minutes.

To make the vinaigrette, open the garlic packets and squeeze the roasted garlic cloves into a blender, squeezing the base of each garlic half. Add the parsley and balsamic vinegar and pulse until blended. Drizzle the oil into the blender while the machine is running. Add the sugar, salt, pepper, and 2 tablespoons water and blend until incorporated.

Slice the pork into ¾-inch-thick slices and transfer to a serving platter. Drizzle some of the vinaigrette over the pork and pass the remaining vinaigrette alongside in a small dish.

Swordfish Poached in Olive Oil with Broccoli Rabe Pesto

I first had oil-poached fish in Napa Valley and loved the way this cooking method kept the fish so moist; you can't really dry it out. You could prepare halibut or just about any other mild white fish this way. Be sure to use a mix of olive and vegetable oils to poach the fish; if you use 100 percent olive oil it will become too bitter. This is another really good-looking dish, with lots of pretty colors.

4 servings

Broccoli Rabe Pesto

- 8 ounces broccoli rabe (about ½ bunch), thick stems removed
- 2 garlic cloves
- 1 cup toasted walnuts (see Note, page 21)
- 1 tablespoon honey
- 1 teaspoon salt
- ½ teaspoon freshly ground black pepper
- ½ cup extra-virgin olive oil
- ¼ cup freshly grated Parmesan cheese

Olive Oil–Poached Swordfish

- 4 cups olive oil
- 2 cups vegetable oil
- 4 (6-ounce) skinless swordfish steaks, each 1-inch thick
- Salt and freshly ground black pepper

To make the pesto, bring a medium pot of salted water to a boil over high heat. Add the broccoli rabe and cook until tender, about 5 minutes. Transfer the cooked broccoli rabe to a large bowl of ice water and let cool, about 3 minutes. Shake off the excess water and transfer to a food processor. Add the garlic, walnuts, honey, salt, and pepper and process until very smooth. With the machine running, gradually pour in the extra-virgin olive oil. Transfer the pesto to a small bowl and stir in the Parmesan. Cover and set aside.

To poach the fish, combine the olive oil and vegetable oil in a Dutch oven or large, deep saucepan big enough to hold the fish in a single layer. Using a deep-fry thermometer, heat the oil to 200°F over medium-low heat. Reduce the heat to low to sustain the 200°F temperature. Season the fish with salt and pepper. Gently place the fish in the oil, making sure it is submerged. Poach the fish until just cooked through, 6 to 7 minutes.

Place about ½ cup of broccoli rabe pesto on each serving plate and gently smooth it out to make a bed for the fish. Using a slotted fish spatula, gently transfer the cooked fish from the poaching oil to the serving plate, placing the fish on top of the bed of pesto. Serve immediately.

Grilled Shrimp in Artichoke Tomato Broth

This is something like a chunky seafood stew, but it's lighter thanks to a bigger dose of veggies and herbs. You can make this with any fish you like in place of the shrimp.

4 servings

Shrimp

- 2 garlic cloves, minced
- 2 teaspoons chopped fresh rosemary leaves
- 3 tablespoons extra-virgin olive oil
- ¼ teaspoon fine sea salt
- ¼ teaspoon freshly ground black pepper
- 1 pound large shrimp, peeled and deveined

Artichoke Tomato Broth

- 3 tablespoons olive oil
- 2 shallots, sliced into thin rounds
- 2 garlic cloves, minced
- 1 pound frozen artichokes, thawed
- ½ cup dry white wine
- 1½ cups low-sodium chicken broth
- 1 (14.5-ounce) can diced tomatoes
- ½ teaspoon minced fresh thyme leaves
- ¼ teaspoon salt
- ¼ teaspoon freshly ground black pepper

Start by marinating the shrimp. Place the garlic, rosemary, extra-virgin olive oil, salt, and pepper in a medium bowl. Add the shrimp and toss until the shrimp are well coated with the mixture. Cover and refrigerate for 1½ hours.

To make the broth, in a medium saucepan, heat the 3 tablespoons of olive oil over medium-high heat. Add the shallots and cook for 1 minute. Add the garlic and artichokes and cook until golden brown, 8 to 10 minutes. Add the white wine and stir, scraping the brown bits off the bottom of the pan with a wooden spoon. Add the chicken broth, tomatoes and their juices, thyme, and salt and pepper, and bring to a boil. Reduce the heat and simmer for 5 minutes.

While the broth simmers, place a ridged grill pan over medium-high heat. Grill the shrimp until just cooked through, 1 to 2 minutes per side.

Ladle the artichoke tomato broth into shallow bowls. Top with the grilled shrimp and serve immediately.

Salmon with Puff Pastry and Pesto

Looking for fancy food made really easy? Look no farther.
For this suave little number the pesto is purchased and the
puff pastry is from the freezer. You will be amazed at what
a spectacular dish you can make in about fifteen minutes with
just five ingredients.

4 servings

1 sheet frozen puff pastry, thawed
2 (10- to 12-ounce) center-cut salmon
  fillets
Salt and pepper to taste
¼ cup sliced almonds
¼ cup purchased pesto
2 tomatoes, sliced

Preheat the oven to 400°F. Line a baking sheet with aluminum foil.

Unfold the puff pastry sheet on a cutting board and use a sharp paring knife to cut 4 4½-inch squares. Prick each square all over with the tines of a fork. Arrange the pastry squares on one end of the baking sheet, about 1 inch apart. Cut the salmon fillets in half crosswise to make 4 pieces about 3 inches square. Season the salmon fillets with salt and pepper and arrange them on the other end of the sheet. Sprinkle each piece of salmon with 1 tablespoon of the sliced almonds. Bake for 10 to 12 minutes, or until the pastry is puffed and golden brown and the salmon is firm.

To serve, place a piece of puff pastry on each plate. Top the pastry with 1 tablespoon of the pesto. Arrange 2 slices of tomato over the pesto and top with the salmon. Serve immediately.

Roasted Halibut with Grapefruit Fennel Salsa

When I meet with fans I often hear this recipe mentioned as a favorite. People really seem to enjoy the bright combination of flavors in the salsa topping.

4 servings

2 ruby red grapefruits
1 fennel bulb, trimmed
¼ cup extra-virgin olive oil
2 tablespoons pitted Niçoise olives, halved
2 tablespoons chopped fresh flat-leaf parsley leaves
1 teaspoon salt
⅛ teaspoon red pepper flakes
4 (6-ounce) pieces halibut
¼ teaspoon freshly ground black pepper

Preheat the oven to 375°F.

With a zester or fine grater, remove 1 teaspoon of zest from one of the grapefruits. Use a large, sharp knife to trim away all the peel and pith from both grapefruits. Hold the peeled fruit over a bowl and cut in between the membranes to free the grapefruit segments; you should have about 1 cup. Squeeze the membranes over the bowl to extract the juice; you want ¼ cup. (Reserve any extra for another use.) Add the zest and segments to the bowl.

Halve the fennel bulb lengthwise, slice it thin, and add it to the bowl with the grapefruit segments. Add the olive oil, olives, parsley, ½ teaspoon of the salt, and the red pepper flakes. Stir to combine.

Meanwhile, place the fish on a parchment-lined roasting dish. Sprinkle with the remaining ½ teaspoon of salt and the black pepper and bake for 10 to 12 minutes depending on thickness.

Gently transfer the fish to a serving plate. Top with the grapefruit and fennel salsa and serve immediately.

Salmon in Lemon Brodetto with Pea Purée

This dish is a perfect embodiment of the way I like to eat. The colors just say spring, it's light, and everything tastes really fresh and bright.

4 servings

Lemon Brodetto

2 tablespoons olive oil
1 shallot, diced
2 lemons, one zested and both juiced
2 cups low-sodium chicken broth
1 tablespoon chopped fresh mint leaves

Pea Purée

2 cups frozen peas, thawed (about 10 ounces)
¼ cup fresh mint leaves
1 garlic clove
½ teaspoon kosher salt
½ teaspoon freshly ground black pepper
½ cup extra-virgin olive oil
½ cup freshly grated Parmesan cheese

Salmon

¼ cup olive oil
4 (4- to 6-ounce) salmon fillets
Kosher salt and freshly ground black pepper

To make the lemon brodetto, warm the olive oil in a medium saucepan over medium heat. Add the shallot and sauté until tender, about 7 minutes. Add the lemon zest and juice, and the broth. Bring to a simmer, cover, and keep warm over low heat.

To make the pea purée, combine the peas, mint, garlic, salt, and pepper in a food processor and purée. With the machine running, add the extra-virgin olive oil in a steady drizzle. Transfer the pea purée to a small bowl and stir in the Parmesan. Set aside.

To make the salmon, warm the olive oil in a large, heavy skillet over high heat. Season the salmon pieces with salt and pepper. Sear the salmon on one side until a golden crust forms, 4 to 5 minutes. Flip the fish and continue cooking until medium-rare, about 2 minutes more depending on the thickness of the fish.

To assemble the dish, stir the tablespoon of chopped mint into the lemon brodetto and divide among 4 shallow bowls. Place a large spoonful of pea purée in the center of each bowl. Place a salmon piece atop each mound of pea purée and serve immediately.

Desserts

STRAWBERRY AND MASCARPONE GRANITA
CHOCOLATE PANNA COTTA WITH AMARETTO WHIPPED CREAM
CITRUS SEMIFREDDO
ESPRESSO CHOCOLATE MOUSSE WITH ORANGE MASCARPONE WHIPPED CREAM
RICOTTA CAPPUCCINO
ORANGE AND CHOCOLATE ZEPPOLE
ALMOND, PINE NUT, AND APRICOT COFFEE CAKE
AMARETTI TORTA
RICOTTA ORANGE POUND CAKE WITH STRAWBERRIES
LEMON RICOTTA COOKIES WITH LEMON GLAZE
CHOCOLATE HAZELNUT BISCOTTI
BERRY STRATA
CORNMEAL AND ROSEMARY CAKE WITH BALSAMIC SYRUP
HAZELNUT CRUNCH CAKE WITH MASCARPONE AND CHOCOLATE

DESSERTS

It's no secret that I have a huge sweet tooth—you might even say I'm a dessert addict. Although Italian cuisine isn't renowned for its desserts the way, say, French chefs are, it's still my favorite course of any meal, and seemingly becoming the favorite of my audience, too. Italian desserts are generally unpretentious, simple to make, and equally easy to fall in love with. What's not to adore about little doughnuts dipped in chocolate sauce? The mixture of chocolate and orange makes them heavenly, and I don't know many people who can resist a warm, sweet doughnut. Creamy Strawberry and Mascarpone Granita is a light but creamy icy dessert and almost all the prep time is in the freezing. From a lemony semifreddo topped with cookie crumbs to a showstopper of a cake with a shortcut secret, these sweet surprises will end any meal on a high note and send your guests home with smiles on their faces.

Strawberry and Mascarpone Granita

I love the flavor of granitas but the texture is usually quite granular and icy; the mascarpone smoothes this version out so it is more like a sherbet. Don't scrape it until just before you serve it, as it will melt and look less appetizing.

4 to 6 servings

½ cup plus 1 tablespoon sugar
½ cup chopped fresh mint leaves
2 cups coarsely chopped strawberries, plus 1 cup finely diced strawberries
½ cup mascarpone cheese
3 tablespoons freshly squeezed lemon juice
Pinch of salt

Place ½ cup of the sugar and the mint in a small pan with 1 cup of water and bring to a simmer, stirring occasionally to help dissolve the sugar. Let simmer over low heat for 5 minutes to steep the mint. Then strain the mint from the simple syrup. Discard the mint.

In a food processor, combine the 2 cups of coarsely chopped strawberries with the remaining 1 tablespoon of sugar. Run the machine to purée the strawberries. Add the mascarpone, lemon juice, and salt and process until the mascarpone is fully incorporated. Add the mint syrup and combine. Pour the strawberry mixture into an 8 x 8-inch glass dish, cover the dish with plastic wrap, and place in the freezer. The mixture will take about 4 hours to freeze.

To serve, use a fork to scrape the granita. Spoon the mixture into chilled bowls. Top with the finely diced strawberries. Serve immediately.

Chocolate Panna Cotta with Amaretto Whipped Cream

This is the chocolate lover's answer to panna cotta. It's quite similar to a mousse but the gelatin makes it a bit firmer.

4 to 6 servings

2 cups cold whole milk

1 cup granulated sugar

1 teaspoon pure vanilla extract

1 packet unflavored gelatin

4 eggs, lightly beaten

1 (12-ounce) bag bittersweet chocolate chips

¼ cup toasted sliced almonds (see Note, page 33)

1 cup whipping cream

1 tablespoon confectioners' sugar

1 tablespoon almond liqueur such as Amaretto

Preheat the oven to 350°F. Butter a 2-quart casserole dish.

In a small saucepan, combine 1½ cups of the milk, the granulated sugar, and the vanilla. Bring to a simmer and stir until the sugar is dissolved. Remove from the heat.

In a small bowl, sprinkle the gelatin over the remaining ½ cup of cold milk and let it dissolve for 2 minutes. Combine the cold milk and gelatin with the hot milk and sugar. Stir to dissolve the gelatin, about 5 minutes. (Heat the milk gently if the gelatin is not dissolving easily.) When the gelatin is dissolved, combine the eggs with the warm milk mixture, whisking constantly to avoid scrambling the eggs. Pour the mixture through a fine-mesh strainer into a large measuring cup or small pitcher.

Meanwhile, melt the chocolate over simmering water in a double boiler. When the chocolate is melted, gradually combine the milk and egg mixture with the melted chocolate, stirring between each addition to create a smooth chocolate mixture.

Pour the mixture into the prepared dish. Sprinkle the top with the almonds. Place the casserole dish in a larger baking pan or roasting pan and add hot water to the larger pan until the water comes halfway up the sides of the casserole dish. Place both pans in the oven and bake the panna cotta until the sides are firm and the center just jiggles slightly, about 1 hour. Remove from the oven and let cool for at least 30 minutes.

Just before serving, whip the cream to soft peaks in a medium bowl using a whisk or electric hand mixer. Add the confectioners' sugar and almond liqueur and whip to combine. Spoon the panna cotta into individual serving bowls and dollop the top with the almond whipped cream.

Citrus Semifreddo

If you have always wanted to try making ice cream at home but haven't wanted to invest in an ice-cream maker, give this recipe a try. Semifreddo is a very rich, creamy dessert, but the lemon juice and limoncello make this one seem very light, despite all the egg yolks and cream.

8 servings

¾ cup sugar
8 large egg yolks
¼ cup freshly squeezed lemon juice
3 tablespoons freshly squeezed lime juice
2 tablespoons limoncello
Pinch of salt
Zest of 1 lemon
Zest of 1 lime
1 cup heavy cream
2 ounces amaretti cookies (about 10 small cookies), crushed

Spray a 9 x 5 x 3-inch metal loaf pan with nonstick cooking spray. Line the pan with plastic wrap, allowing the excess to hang over the ends and sides.

Whisk ½ cup of the sugar, the egg yolks, lemon juice, lime juice, limoncello, and salt in a large metal bowl to blend. Stir in the zests. Set the bowl over a saucepan of simmering water (do not allow the bottom of the bowl to touch the water). Whisk the egg mixture until it is thick and creamy, and a thermometer inserted into the mixture registers 160°F, about 5 minutes. Set the bowl of custard into another bowl of ice water to cool completely.

Using an electric mixer, beat the cream and remaining ¼ cup sugar in another large bowl until firm peaks form. Using a large rubber spatula, gently fold the whipped cream into the custard. Spoon the mixture into the prepared loaf pan. Fold the overhanging plastic wrap over the custard and freeze until frozen, at least 8 hours or up to 3 days.

Unfold the plastic wrap. Invert the semifreddo onto a platter and peel off the plastic wrap. Cut the semifreddo into 1-inch-thick slices, sprinkle with the cookie crumbs, and serve.

Espresso Chocolate Mousse with Orange Mascarpone Whipped Cream

If you're intimidated by the prospect of making a mousse, this recipe is pretty cool. Once you've warmed up the milk, just combine everything in the blender, then pop it in the fridge to chill. Desserts don't get any easier than that. Top individual servings with any kind of flavored cream you like; I like orange with chocolate, but a cinnamon cream would be nice, too.

4 servings

Mousse
½ cup whole milk
3 tablespoons granulated sugar
¼ teaspoon instant espresso powder
1 cup bittersweet chocolate chips
3 large egg whites

Orange Mascarpone Whipped Cream
¼ cup mascarpone cheese, at room temperature
2 tablespoons freshly squeezed orange juice
½ cup heavy cream
2 tablespoons confectioners' sugar
1 teaspoon grated orange zest

To make the mousse, in a small saucepan stir the milk together with the granulated sugar and the espresso powder over medium heat until the milk is hot, but not boiling, and the sugar is dissolved.

Place the chocolate chips in a blender. Pour the hot milk over the chips. Run the blender on high until combined, just a few seconds, then add the egg whites and run the blender on high until light, about 1 minute. Transfer the mousse to 4 small serving cups. Cover with plastic wrap and refrigerate until firm, about 3 hours.

To make the mascarpone whipped cream, in the bowl of an electric mixer stir together the mascarpone and the orange juice until smooth. Add the cream, confectioners' sugar, and orange zest. Whip until the cream forms soft peaks, about 1 minute.

Spoon a dollop of the whipped cream onto each mousse and serve.

Note: This recipe includes raw egg whites, which are not recommended for children, the elderly, or those with compromised immune systems. If you have health concerns about raw eggs, choose a different recipe.

The mascarpone whipped cream can be made several hours ahead of time and stored, covered with plastic wrap, in the refrigerator.

Ricotta Cappuccino

Comfort food meets the espresso bar in these cute little cups of sweetness. Not quite a pudding, the mixture is frothy and thick, like the crema that tops a good cup of cappuccino.

4 servings

½ cup sugar
½ vanilla bean
1 (15-ounce) container whole-milk ricotta cheese
1½ teaspoons instant espresso powder
1 (3-inch) biscotti, crushed
Pinch of ground cinnamon
Pinch of cocoa powder

Place the sugar in a food processor. Cut the vanilla bean open lengthwise and scrape the seeds into the food processor with the sugar. Pulse to combine well. Add the ricotta and espresso powder and blend for 1 minute. Stop the machine to scrape down the sides with a rubber spatula, then blend for another minute. Spoon the mixture into 4 small coffee mugs. Cover and refrigerate for at least 1 hour and up to 1 day.

To serve, top the ricotta cappuccino with crushed biscotti. Sprinkle with cinnamon and cocoa powder.

Orange and Chocolate Zeppole

Zeppole are little doughnuts that are sold on the street in Naples and at street fairs. They are usually served with a simple dusting of powdered sugar, but the combination of chocolate and orange in this version is just to die for. Eat these warm, because they become heavy and doughy once they cool (if they stay around that long!).

4 to 6 servings

Chocolate Sauce
¾ cup heavy cream
1 cup bittersweet chocolate chips

Orange Zeppole
½ cup (1 stick) unsalted butter
¼ cup sugar
¼ teaspoon salt
1 cup all-purpose flour
4 eggs
1 tablespoon grated orange zest
Vegetable oil, for frying

Orange Sugar
1 tablespoon grated orange zest
½ cup sugar

For the chocolate sauce, heat the cream in a small saucepan until hot but not boiling. Combine the cream and chocolate in a heat-proof bowl and stir until smooth.

For the orange zeppole, combine the butter, sugar, salt, and ½ cup water in a medium saucepan and bring to a boil over medium heat. Take the pan off the heat and stir in the flour. Return the pan to low heat and cook, stirring continuously, until the mixture forms a ball, about 4 minutes. Transfer the flour mixture to a medium bowl. Using an electric hand mixer on low speed, beat in the eggs, one at a time, incorporating each egg completely before adding the next. Add the orange zest and beat until smooth. Set aside.

For the orange sugar, place the orange zest and sugar in a food processor. Pulse until the mixture is blended. Transfer the sugar to a shallow dish and set aside.

Pour enough oil into a large frying pan to reach a depth of 2 inches. Heat the oil over medium heat until a deep-fry thermometer registers 350°F.

Using a small ice-cream scoop or 2 small spoons, carefully drop about a tablespoon of the dough into the hot oil. Make three more zeppole, being careful to not crowd the pan. Turn each zeppole once or twice, cooking until golden and puffed, about 5 minutes. Roll the cooked zeppoles with the orange sugar, then transfer to a plate. Continue frying the remaining batter in batchs of 4.

Reheat the chocolate sauce if necessary, and serve in a small bowl with the zeppole.

Almond, Pine Nut, and Apricot Coffee Cake

Believe it or not, cakes like this one, featuring nuts and dried fruits, are very popular in Venice. There it would be considered an afternoon snack to serve with coffee, but it's wonderful for breakfast as well.

6 to 8 servings

½ cup sliced almonds
½ cup pine nuts
1¼ cups all-purpose flour
1 teaspoon baking powder
½ teaspoon salt
4 large eggs
1¼ cups sugar
¾ cup (1½ sticks) unsalted butter, melted
⅓ cup milk
¼ teaspoon almond extract
½ cup dried apricots, chopped

Preheat the oven to 350°F. Butter and flour a 9-inch cake pan.

Combine ¼ cup of the almonds and ¼ cup of the pine nuts in a dry skillet and place over medium-high heat, stirring occasionally, until lightly browned and toasted, about 10 minutes. Transfer to a food processor and cool for a few minutes, then pulse until the nuts are finely ground. Transfer the nuts to a medium bowl, add the flour, baking powder, and salt, and stir to combine. Set aside.

In a medium bowl, use an electric mixer to beat the eggs and the sugar until the mixture is thick and pale yellow. Add the butter and milk and combine, then stir in the almond extract and apricots by hand. Gently stir in the dry ingredients.

Pour the batter into the prepared cake pan. Sprinkle the top of the cake with the remaining ¼ cup of sliced almonds and ¼ cup of pine nuts. Bake until the cake is cooked and a toothpick inserted in the middle comes out clean, 50 to 55 minutes. Let the cake cool on a wire rack. Use a knife to loosen the edges. Turn the cake out, cut in wedges, and serve.

Amaretti Torta

Here's another recipe in which just a few ingredients come together to make a big, big impression. It's not as dense as the name suggests, because the beaten egg whites lighten it up considerably, as do the crumbled cookies. Think of this next time you're looking for an unusual birthday cake; with its layer of marmalade and crumbled cookie topping it's elegant enough for any important occasion.

8 to 10 servings

20 whole amaretti cookies, plus 8 amaretti cookies, crushed, for topping
½ cup semisweet chocolate chips
1 cup (2 sticks) unsalted butter, at room temperature
1 cup sugar
5 large eggs, separated
2 tablespoons orange-flavored liqueur (Triple Sec, Cointreau, or Grand Marnier)
½ cup all-purpose flour
¼ cup orange marmalade

Preheat the oven to 350°F. Grease a 10-inch cake pan and line the bottom with a circle of parchment paper.

Combine the 20 amaretti cookies and the chocolate chips in a food processor and process until the mixture is very finely chopped. Set aside.

Using an electric mixer and a large bowl, cream together the butter and sugar until pale yellow, about 2 minutes. Add the egg yolks one at a time, incorporating each yolk before adding the next. Once all the eggs are added, continue to cream the mixture together until light and fluffy, about 4 more minutes. Add the orange liqueur. With the machine on low, add the flour and the chocolate amaretti mixture, mixing well after each addition.

In a medium bowl, whip the egg whites (using the electric mixer and clean beaters) until stiff peaks form, about 3 minutes. Add one third of the whipped egg whites to the batter and mix until combined. Gently fold the remaining egg whites into the batter until just barely combined. Pour the batter into the prepared cake pan. Bake until a toothpick inserted in the center comes out clean, 45 to 50 minutes.

Let the cake cool in the pan on a wire rack for 10 minutes. Turn the cake out onto a platter and cool to room temperature. Spread the orange marmalade over the top of the cake in an even layer, and sprinkle with the remaining crushed amaretti cookies.

Ricotta Orange Pound Cake with Strawberries

Pound cakes are perennially popular because they are such good keepers; this one will keep in the freezer for up to six months if it's tightly wrapped. Pull it out and dress it up or dress it down; it's great either way.

6 to 8 servings

1½ cups cake flour
2½ teaspoons baking powder
1 teaspoon kosher salt
¾ cup (1½ sticks) unsalted butter, at room temperature, plus more to grease the baking pan
1½ cups whole-milk ricotta cheese
1½ cups plus 1 tablespoon granulated sugar
3 large eggs
1 teaspoon pure vanilla extract
Zest of 1 orange
2 tablespoons Amaretto
Confectioners' sugar, for dusting
1 pint strawberries, hulled and quartered

Preheat the oven to 350°F. Grease a 9 x 5 x 3-inch loaf pan with butter.

In a medium bowl, combine the flour, baking powder, and salt. Stir to combine.

Using an electric mixer, cream together the butter, ricotta, and the 1½ cups of granulated sugar until light and fluffy, about 3 minutes. Add the eggs one at a time, beating until each is incorporated before adding the next. Add the vanilla, orange zest, and Amaretto and mix until combined. Add the dry ingredients, a small amount at a time, beating just until incorporated.

Pour the mixture into the prepared pan and bake until a toothpick comes out clean and the cake is beginning to pull away from the sides of the pan, 45 to 50 minutes. Let the cake cool in the pan for 10 minutes, then turn out onto a wire rack to cool completely. Using a sieve, dust the cooled cake with confectioners' sugar.

Meanwhile, place the strawberries in a small bowl with the remaining 1 tablespoon of granulated sugar. Toss to combine, then set aside until the strawberries have released some of their juices.

To serve, slice the cake and serve topped with a spoonful of strawberries and their juices.

Lemon Ricotta Cookies with Lemon Glaze

More cakey than crispy, these ladylike little tea cakes puff up as they bake, almost like little muffin tops. The lemon glaze on top adds a tart, crunchy layer.

Makes 44 cookies

2½ cups all-purpose flour
1 teaspoon baking powder
1 teaspoon salt
½ cup (1 stick) unsalted butter, at room temperature
2 cups granulated sugar
2 eggs
1 (15-ounce) container whole-milk ricotta cheese
Zest of 1 lemon
3 tablespoons freshly squeezed lemon juice

Glaze

1½ cups confectioners' sugar
Zest of 1 lemon
3 tablespoons freshly squeezed lemon juice

Preheat the oven to 375°F.

In a medium bowl, combine the flour, baking powder, and salt. Set aside.

In a large bowl, using an electric mixer, beat the butter and granulated sugar until light and fluffy, about 3 minutes. Add the eggs, 1 at a time, beating until incorporated. Add the ricotta cheese, lemon zest, and lemon juice and beat to combine. Stir in the dry ingredients.

Line 2 baking sheets with parchment paper. Spoon the dough onto the baking sheets using about 2 tablespoons for each cookie. Bake for 15 minutes, until slightly golden at the edges. Remove from the oven and let the cookies rest on the baking sheet for 20 minutes.

While they cool, combine the confectioners' sugar, lemon zest, and lemon juice in a small bowl and stir until smooth. Spoon about ½ teaspoon of the glaze onto each cooled cookie and use the back of the spoon to spread it to the edges. Let the glaze harden for about 2 hours. Pack the cookies in an airtight container.

Chocolate Hazelnut Biscotti

Anytime I can find a way to incorporate Nutella into a recipe, I will. These treats are what my grandmother used to make and referred to as "biscotti." So in keeping with her tradition, I'll do the same, even though these are more like a drop cookie, more buttery and moist than the usual biscotti, which are generally quite hard and dry.

Makes 36 cookies

1⅓ cups all-purpose flour
½ teaspoon baking powder
½ teaspoon baking soda
¼ teaspoon kosher salt
½ cup (1 stick) unsalted butter, at room temperature
½ cup chocolate hazelnut spread such as Nutella
½ cup granulated sugar
½ cup light brown sugar
1 egg
1 teaspoon pure vanilla extract
¾ cup chopped toasted, skinless hazelnuts (see Note)

Preheat the oven to 375°F. Line a cookie sheet with parchment paper.

In a medium bowl, combine the flour, baking powder, baking soda, and salt. Set aside.

In another medium bowl, using an electric mixer, cream the butter, chocolate hazelnut spread, and both sugars together, about 4 minutes. Add the egg and vanilla and beat until smooth, about 1 minute. Using a wooden spoon or rubber spatula, stir in the flour mixture until just combined. Add the hazelnuts and stir until just combined.

Using a tablespoon measure, drop spoonfuls of the cookie dough onto the cookie sheet, spacing the mounds about 4 inches apart. Use the tines of a fork to flatten each mound. Bake 10 to 12 minutes. Use a metal spatula to transfer the cookies to a wire rack and let cool.

Note: To toast the hazelnuts, spread them on a baking sheet and place in a 350°F oven for 8 to 10 minutes, or until golden and fragrant.

Berry Strata

Essentially a berry bread pudding, the ricotta and eggs in this dessert make it substantial and rich enough to serve for brunch. Serve with a side of maple syrup for breakfast, or a dollop of lightly sweetened whipped cream for dessert.

6 to 8 servings

2 tablespoons (¼ stick) unsalted butter
3 tablespoons honey
4 large eggs
½ cup whole-milk ricotta cheese
3 tablespoons sugar
1 cup whole milk
¼ cup freshly squeezed orange juice
4 slices bread, torn into 1-inch pieces (about 4 cups)
1 (10-ounce) bag frozen mixed berries, thawed and drained

Melt the butter in a small saucepan over low heat. Turn off the heat, add the honey, and stir to combine.

Combine the eggs, ricotta, and sugar in a large bowl. Using a fork, mix to combine and beat the eggs. Add the milk, orange juice, butter and honey mixture, and bread. Stir to combine. Gently fold in the berries.

Pour the mixture into a 10-inch round (2-quart) baking dish. Cover with plastic wrap and place in the refrigerator for at least 2 hours and up to 12 hours.

Preheat the oven to 350°F. Bake the strata until golden on top and baked through, about 40 minutes. Let stand for 5 minutes before serving. Spoon into dishes and serve.

Cornmeal and Rosemary Cake with Balsamic Syrup

Imagine the best corn muffin you've ever tasted, but richer and sweeter. The rosemary adds a subtle flavor and aroma that is reminiscent of the holidays. It's equally nice with a cup of tea or a glass of dessert wine. Balsamic syrup is mellow and intense with an almost chocolatey flavor that complements the rosemary.

4 to 6 servings

Cake

- ½ cup fine yellow cornmeal
- ½ cup cake flour
- 1 tablespoon minced fresh rosemary leaves
- 1 teaspoon baking powder
- ¼ teaspoon salt
- ½ cup (1 stick) unsalted butter, at room temperature
- ½ teaspoon pure vanilla extract
- 1¼ cups confectioners' sugar, plus more for dusting
- 4 large egg yolks
- 2 large eggs
- ½ cup sour cream

Balsamic Syrup

- ½ cup granulated sugar
- ½ cup balsamic vinegar
- ½ small fresh rosemary sprig

Preheat the oven to 350°F. Butter and flour an 8-inch round cake pan.

In a medium bowl whisk together the cornmeal, cake flour, minced rosemary, baking powder, and salt.

Using a stand mixer with a paddle attachment, beat the butter and vanilla together on low speed until combined. Slowly add the confectioners' sugar. Once the sugar is incorporated, increase the speed to high and beat until fluffy, about 3 minutes. Add the egg yolks and eggs 1 at a time, beating until each is incorporated before adding the next. Reduce the speed to medium and add the sour cream. On low speed, add the dry ingredients and mix just until incorporated.

Pour the batter into the prepared cake pan and smooth the surface with a spatula. Bake in the lower third of the oven until the cake is golden and pulls away from the sides of the pan, about 35 minutes. Transfer the pan to a wire rack and let cool.

While the cake bakes, make the balsamic syrup. Combine the sugar, balsamic vinegar, and rosemary in a small saucepan. Bring to a boil and simmer until the sugar is dissolved, about 5 minutes. Discard the rosemary sprig and let the syrup cool.

Transfer the cake from the pan to a serving plate and dust with confectioners' sugar. Serve drizzled with the balsamic syrup.

Hazelnut Crunch Cake with Mascarpone and Chocolate

A lot of steps go into putting this cake together but since it starts with a boxed cake mix, none of them is very difficult. All the effort goes into the creamy-crunchy filling, made from hazelnut brittle that is a delicious candy all on its own. It makes for a spectacular birthday cake.

8 servings

Cake

- 1 box chocolate cake mix and any additonal ingredients needed to make the cake

Crunch

- 1 cup (about 4½ ounces) hazelnuts, toasted and skinned (see Note, page 190)
- ⅔ cup granulated sugar

Filling

- 2 (8-ounce) containers mascarpone cheese, at room temperature
- 1 cup heavy cream
- ¾ cup confectioners' sugar
- 1 teaspoon pure vanilla extract

Topping

- ¼ cup bittersweet chocolate chips
- 1 tablespoon granulated sugar
- 1 teaspoon grated orange zest

Preheat the oven to 350°F. Butter and flour two 8-inch cake pans.

Prepare the cake mix according to package instructions. Divide the batter between the cake pans and bake as directed. Remove from the oven and cool on a wire rack.

To make the crunch, place the toasted nuts close together in a single layer on a parchment-lined baking sheet. Combine the granulated sugar and ⅓ cup of water in a small saucepan. Bring to a boil over medium-high heat and stir until the sugar has dissolved. Continue to boil the mixture until the sugar is light brown, about 8 minutes. Remove from the heat and let the bubbles subside, then pour the caramelized sugar over the nuts. Place the baking sheet in the refrigerator and let the nut crunch cool until hard, about 30 minutes. When the nut crunch is hardened and cool, place it on a cutting board and cut into small pieces, saving a few larger ones for decoration. Set aside.

To make the filling, put the mascarpone, cream, confectioners' sugar, and vanilla into a large mixing bowl. Using an electric mixer, whip the cream mixture to soft peaks. Fold the chopped nut crunch into the whipped cream.

To make the topping, place the chocolate chips, granulated sugar, and zest in a food processor. Process the mixture until the chocolate is finely ground.

To assemble the cake, put 1 cake layer on a serving plate or cake stand. Top with a 1-inch layer of the whipped cream–hazelnut crunch filling. Place the second layer of cake on top of the first and frost the entire cake with the remaining filling. Sprinkle the top and sides of the cake with the ground chocolate topping and add some shards of nut crunch as decoration. Serve.

(Not) Just for Kids

POLENTA-CRUSTED SHRIMP WITH HONEY MUSTARD

PARMESAN FISH STICKS

MINI CALZONES

PROSCIUTTO MOZZARELLA PINWHEELS

ORECCHIETTE WITH MINI CHICKEN MEATBALLS

FUSILLI ALLA CAPRESE

ORZO WITH SAUSAGE, PEPPERS, AND TOMATOES

PIZZA POT PIES

SWEET AND STICKY CHICKEN DRUMSTICKS

MASCARPONE MINI CUPCAKES WITH STRAWBERRY GLAZE

GRILLED SUMMER FRUIT

CHOCOLATE CHIP POUND CAKE

ITALIAN ICE

(NOT) JUST FOR KIDS

These days I find that lots and lots of kids are interested in and excited about food and cooking, and I couldn't be more thrilled that I can play even a small part in inspiring them to learn about food and to make better decisions about what they eat. Over the years, some of my most popular recipes have been those I've written for kids, dishes they can either make themselves (with the help of an adult, of course) or are just trustworthy go-tos for those young, discerning palates. Either way, my hope is that these recipes will help kids be more comfortable in the kitchen and give them the confidence to try new foods, and to ultimately create their own dishes.

To get them started, I've rounded up a selection of recipes that will please young and old. I found that many kids love meatballs, and the chicken meatballs in this chapter are lighter on kids' tummies and yummier than regular ones; mixed with orecchiette pasta, they are simply fun to eat. Kids and adults alike love pizza and chicken pot pie, so I combined the two in a ramekin full of lots of goodies with an easy, cheesy pizza crust. Whichever you choose, you're *all* guaranteed to have fun in the kitchen.

Polenta-Crusted Shrimp
with Honey Mustard

The polenta coating on these fried shrimp makes a shell-like exterior that is just irresistible. I like this with honey mustard for dipping; but if you want to dip yours in marinara or even ketchup, you have my permission. Don't worry about the paprika; it gives a bit of color but not any heat.

4 to 6 servings

Polenta-Crusted Shrimp

Vegetable cooking spray
½ cup all-purpose flour
2 eggs, beaten
1½ cups fine polenta
2 teaspoons sweet paprika
1 pound large shrimp, peeled and
   deveined, tail on
Kosher salt, for sprinkling

Honey Mustard Sauce

½ cup Dijon mustard
2 tablespoons plain yogurt
5 tablespoons honey

To make the shrimp, position an oven rack in the center of the oven and preheat to 475°F. Coat a baking sheet liberally with vegetable cooking spray.

Put the flour in a small bowl. Pour the beaten eggs into another small bowl. Mix together the polenta and paprika in a medium bowl. Working in batches, dredge the shrimp in the flour. Dip the flour-dredged shrimp into the eggs and then coat with the polenta mixture.

Place the shrimp on the prepared baking sheet. Bake for 10 to 12 minutes, until crisp and golden. Sprinkle with the kosher salt.

To make the sauce, combine the honey mustard ingredients in a small bowl and stir until smooth. Serve the shrimp with little dishes of sauce for dipping.

Parmesan Fish Sticks

Even kids who are not big fish-eaters tend to like salmon—
and they'll like it even better when it's baked in a cheesy crumb
coating. Let them do the dipping and crumb coating to speed
the work along. The fish sticks can also be dipped in ketchup,
marinara sauce, pesto, ranch dressing, or vinaigrette if you prefer.

4 to 6 servings

Fish Sticks

1 (18-ounce) skinless center-cut salmon
   fillet, about 9 by 4 inches
½ cup all-purpose flour
½ teaspoon salt
¼ teaspoon freshly ground black pepper
3 egg whites
1 cup freshly grated Parmesan cheese
1 cup seasoned bread crumbs
Olive oil, for pan and drizzling

Dipping Sauce

⅓ cup reduced-fat mayonnaise
⅓ cup plain low-fat yogurt
1 tablespoon Dijon mustard
1 tablespoon chopped fresh flat-leaf
   parsley or chives

Preheat the oven to 450°F.

To make the fish sticks, rinse the salmon
fillet and pat dry with paper towels. Cut the
fish in half to make 2 fillets, each about 4 by
4½ inches. Starting on the longer edge, slice
each piece into ½-inch strips. Cut any very
tall strips in half horizontally so all the pieces
are about ½ by ½ by 4½ inches.

Place the flour in a medium bowl and season
with the salt and pepper. Place the egg whites
in another bowl and beat until frothy, about
30 seconds. Combine the Parmesan and
bread crumbs in a third bowl.

Coat the salmon pieces in the seasoned flour
and pat to remove any excess. Dip the floured
salmon in the egg whites and then into the
bread-crumb mixture, gently pressing the
mixture into the fish. Place the breaded
salmon on a liberally oiled baking sheet and
drizzle lightly with a bit more olive oil. Bake for
15 to 20 minutes, or until golden brown.

To make the dipping sauce, mix the
mayonnaise, yogurt, Dijon mustard, and parsley (or chives, if using) in a small bowl.

Arrange the fish sticks on a serving platter
and serve with the dipping sauce.

Mini Calzones

Calzones are more popular in Italy than in this country, but they are great kid food and are a little easier to eat than a conventional pizza slice. Each one is a little surprise package; stuff whatever you like inside. Let the kids fill, roll, and seal the calzones before you pop them in the oven.

Makes 16 calzones; 4 to 6 servings

1 tablespoon olive oil

8 ounces Italian-style turkey sausage

1 cup tightly packed arugula (about 1 ounce)

4 ounces cream cheese, at room temperature

⅓ cup plus ¼ cup freshly grated Parmesan cheese

½ teaspoon salt

¼ teaspoon freshly ground black pepper

1 (13.5-ounce) tube of refrigerated pizza dough

All-purpose flour, for rolling the dough

1 egg, beaten (for egg wash)

1½ cups marinara sauce, store-bought or homemade (page 144)

Heat the olive oil over medium-high heat in a medium-size, heavy skillet. Add the sausage and cook until crumbled and golden, about 5 minutes. Add the arugula and cook until wilted. Turn off the heat and let cool for about 10 minutes. Add the cream cheese, ⅓ cup of the Parmesan, the salt, and the pepper and stir to combine. Set aside.

Preheat the oven to 400°F. Line a baking sheet with parchment paper.

Roll out the pizza dough on a lightly floured surface to a thin 20 by 12-inch rectangle. Cut the rectangle in half lengthwise, then cut each half into 8 equal rectangles.

Spoon some of the topping onto 1 side of each rectangle. Using a pastry brush, brush the edges of the rectangle with egg wash. Close the rectangle of pizza dough over the topping. Use a fork to seal and crimp the edges. Place the calzones on the prepared baking sheet and brush the top of each with egg wash. Sprinkle with the remaining ¼ cup of Parmesan. Bake until golden, 15 to 17 minutes.

Meanwhile, heat the marinara sauce over low heat in a medium saucepan. Serve the hot calzones with the marinara sauce alongside for dipping.

Prosciutto Mozzarella Pinwheels

I usually make this in one big log because it is so impressive when it comes out of the oven and you cut it into slices, but if the kids are helping put this together, why not make it as four individual rolls? That way everyone can stuff and roll his or her own selections. Let an adult cut the hot rolls, because the yummy molten cheese retains a lot of heat.

6 to 8 servings

Flour, for dusting
1 pound purchased pizza dough
2 cups shredded mozzarella cheese
7 ounces prosciutto, thinly sliced
1 cup coarsely chopped baby spinach
    (about 1½ ounces)
1 tablespoon olive oil
Kosher salt and freshly ground black
    pepper

Preheat the oven to 425°F and position a rack in the lower third of the oven. Line a baking sheet with parchment paper.

On a lightly floured work surface, roll out the pizza dough into a 12- to 14-inch circle, about ¼ inch thick. Sprinkle half of the mozzarella over the dough. Arrange the prosciutto over the cheese in a single layer. Sprinkle with the chopped spinach, then top with the remaining cheese.

Roll the dough into a thin cylinder, gently tucking in the ends. Brush the entire roll with the olive oil and season with the salt and pepper. Place the dough, seam side down, on the baking sheet and bake for 25 minutes, or until the top is golden brown.

Cool the roll for 3 or 4 minutes, then use a serrated knife to cut it into ¾-inch-wide slices.

Orecchiette
with Mini Chicken Meatballs

This is a perfect dish for parents and kids to make together. Let the little ones roll the meat mixture into tiny balls while you sauté each batch and do the knife work. At the end everyone can help stir the pasta, meatballs, and cheese and tomatoes together.

4 to 6 servings

1 pound orecchiette pasta
¼ cup plain bread crumbs
¼ cup chopped fresh flat-leaf parsley
2 large eggs, lightly beaten
1 tablespoon whole milk
1 tablespoon ketchup
¾ cup freshly grated Romano cheese
¾ teaspoon salt
¾ teaspoon freshly ground black pepper
1 pound ground chicken
¼ cup olive oil
1½ cups low-sodium chicken broth
4 cups cherry tomatoes, halved
1 cup freshly grated Parmesan cheese
8 ounces bocconcini (small mozzarella balls), halved
1 cup chopped fresh basil leaves

Bring a large pot of salted water to a boil over high heat. Add the pasta and cook until tender but still firm to the bite, stirring occasionally, 8 to 10 minutes.

In a medium bowl, stir together the bread crumbs, parsley, eggs, milk, ketchup, Romano cheese, salt, and pepper. Add the chicken and combine well. Using a melon baller (or a teaspoon measure) to scoop up the mixture, roll the seasoned chicken into ¾-inch mini meatballs.

Heat the oil in a large skillet over medium-high heat. Working in batches, add the meatballs and cook without moving until brown on the bottom, about 2 minutes. Turn the meatballs and brown the tops, about 2 minutes longer. Add the chicken broth and tomatoes and bring to a boil, using a wooden spoon to scrape up the brown bits that cling to the bottom of the pan. Reduce the heat to low and simmer until the tomatoes are soft and the meatballs are cooked through, about 5 minutes.

Drain the pasta, reserving about 1 cup of the pasta water. Transfer the pasta to a large serving bowl and add ½ cup of the Parmesan. Toss to coat the orecchiette lightly, adding some of the reserved pasta water to help make a sauce. Add the meatball mixture, bocconcini, and ½ cup of the basil and combine. Garnish with the remaining ½ cup of Parmesan and the remaining basil.

Fusilli alla Caprese

If you love caprese salad but want a meal, this will make you very happy. The hot pasta melts the cheese slightly and makes the garlic and basil smell amazing. I can tell you that in my experience most kids *love* this.

4 to 6 servings

1 pound fusilli pasta
3 tablespoons olive oil
2 garlic cloves, minced
3 cups cherry tomatoes, quartered
   (about 1½ pints)
1 teaspoon salt
½ teaspoon freshly ground black pepper
½ cup packed fresh basil leaves, torn
8 ounces fresh mozzarella, diced
   (about 1¼ cups)

Bring a large pot of salted water to a boil over high heat. Add the pasta and cook until tender but still firm to the bite, stirring occasionally, 8 to 10 minutes. Reserve ½ cup of the pasta cooking liquid, then drain the pasta and transfer to a large bowl.

Meanwhile, heat the olive oil in a medium skillet over medium heat. Add the garlic and sauté until fragrant, about 2 minutes. Add the tomatoes, salt, and pepper. As the tomatoes cook and soften, smash them with a fork. Continue to cook until the tomatoes make a chunky sauce, about 4 minutes. Add the tomato sauce to the bowl with the pasta and toss to combine. Stir in the basil leaves and mozzarella, then add the reserved pasta water, ¼ cup at a time, until the pasta is moist. Serve.

Orzo with Sausage, Peppers, and Tomatoes

I always think of dishes made with small pasta shapes like orzo as kid food because they are easy to scoop up with a spoon— no twirling required! This is an all-around crowd-pleaser that seems to satisfy kids of all ages. It's also quite adaptable; if your kids don't like peppers, leave them out and add more tomatoes. Skip the hot peppers if you don't want it too spicy; and feel free to use any kind of sausage your family enjoys.

4 to 6 servings

3 cups chicken broth
1 pound orzo pasta
2 tablespoons olive oil
2 links (7 ounces total) mild Italian turkey sausage, casings removed
1 garlic clove, minced
2 jarred roasted red bell peppers, cut in ¼-inch strips
2 plum tomatoes, chopped
¼ teaspoon red pepper flakes (optional)
2 tablespoons chopped fresh flat-leaf parsley leaves
Salt and freshly ground black pepper
½ cup freshly grated Parmesan cheese

In a large saucepan, bring the chicken broth and 3 cups of water to a boil over high heat. Add the pasta and cook until tender but still firm to the bite, stirring occasionally, 8 to 10 minutes.

While the pasta is cooking, heat the oil in a large skillet over medium-high heat. Add the turkey sausage and sauté until cooked through, about 4 minutes. Add the garlic and cook for 1 minute. Add the bell peppers, tomatoes, and red pepper flakes (if using) to the pan and cook until heated through, about 2 minutes.

Drain the pasta, reserving about ½ cup of the cooking liquid, and transfer it to a large serving bowl. Add the sausage mixture, 1 tablespoon of the parsley, and salt and pepper to taste. Toss well to combine, adding the reserved cooking liquid if needed to loosen the pasta. Top with the Parmesan and sprinkle with the remaining parsley.

Pizza Pot Pies

Here is my version of chicken pot pie, with my twist being the addition of a pizza crust in place of the expected pastry topper. This is the kind of thing you can make for kids or adults: use a slightly larger ramekin for an adult-size serving and serve it with a side salad; or make it in smaller portions for kids and serve with veggie sticks or even French fries.

6 servings

Tomato Sauce

- 1 tablespoon olive oil
- 2 garlic cloves, minced
- 1 teaspoon minced fresh rosemary leaves
- 2 ounces diced pancetta
- 1 (28-ounce) can crushed tomatoes
- ¼ teaspoon salt
- ¼ teaspoon freshly ground black pepper

Pizza Pot Pies

- 3 cups Tomato Sauce (see above)
- 2 cups diced roasted chicken (from a purchased roasted chicken)
- 2 cups broccoli cut into small, bite-size pieces
- 1½ cups diced mozzarella cheese
- ½ teaspoon salt
- ¼ teaspoon freshly ground black pepper
- 1½ pounds purchased pizza dough
- ⅓ cup olive oil
- 6 tablespoons freshly grated Parmesan cheese

Special equipment: 6 (10-ounce) ramekins

To make the tomato sauce, warm the olive oil in a small saucepan over medium heat. Add the garlic, rosemary, and pancetta and sauté until the pancetta is crisp and golden, about 5 minutes. Add the tomatoes, stir to combine, and simmer over very low heat for 15 minutes. Add the salt and pepper. Set aside.

To make the pot pies, preheat the oven to 400°F. In a large bowl, combine the tomato sauce, chicken, broccoli, mozzarella, salt, and pepper. Stir to combine. Divide the chicken mixture evenly among six 10-ounce ramekins. Roll out the pizza dough ½- to ¾-inch thick, and use a paring knife to cut circles that are 1 inch larger in diameter than the ramekins. Set the circles of dough over the filled ramekins and press down to seal, making sure to pull the dough over the edges of each ramekin. Brush the pizza crust with the olive oil and sprinkle with the Parmesan cheese. Cut a small slit in the top with the paring knife. Bake until the pizza crust is golden, about 25 minutes. Remove from the oven and let cool slightly before serving.

Sweet and Sticky Chicken Drumsticks

The kids won't be the only ones licking their fingers when you serve this. My mother made a dish similar to this when I was a kid and we just couldn't get enough of it; the leftovers were my favorite after-school snack, eaten cold right out of the fridge. The rosemary and garlic are subtle but make the flavor a little more complex, and brushing the cooked drumettes with the reduced marinade intensifies the flavors even more.

4 to 6 servings

½ cup balsamic vinegar
½ cup honey
½ cup light brown sugar, packed
¼ cup soy sauce
5 fresh rosemary sprigs
5 garlic cloves, halved
10 to 12 chicken drumsticks
2 tablespoons toasted sesame seeds
¼ cup chopped fresh flat-leaf parsley leaves

Combine the balsamic vinegar, honey, brown sugar, soy sauce, rosemary sprigs, and garlic cloves in a large, resealable plastic bag. Shake and squeeze the contents of the bag to dissolve the honey and the brown sugar. Add the chicken drumsticks to the bag and seal, squeezing out as much air from the bag as possible. Marinate in the refrigerator for 2 hours.

Preheat the oven to 450°F. Line a rimmed baking sheet with aluminum foil.

Remove the chicken drumsticks from the bag, reserving the marinade, and arrange them on the prepared baking sheet. Bake until the skin is caramelized and very dark in spots, 30 to 35 minutes.

Meanwhile, place the marinade in a small saucepan. Bring the marinade to a boil, then reduce the heat to a simmer and cook over low heat until thick, about 15 minutes.

Use a pastry brush to brush some of the cooked marinade on the cooked chicken. Place the chicken on a serving platter. Sprinkle with the sesame seeds and the chopped parsley.

Mascarpone Mini Cupcakes with Strawberry Glaze

Make these for your little girl's next tea party; they are pretty and so easy to make. Or feel free to make these in a regular-size muffin tin, increasing the baking time by about 5 minutes.

Makes 48 mini muffins

8 ounces mascarpone cheese, at room temperature
2 egg whites
¼ cup vegetable oil
1 box white cake mix
⅓ cup frozen strawberries, thawed and drained
2½ cups confectioners' sugar

Preheat the oven to 350°F. Line 4 mini muffin tins (a total of 48 mini muffin molds) with paper liners.

In a large bowl, combine the mascarpone, egg whites, and vegetable oil. Using a hand mixer, beat the ingredients until combined and creamy. Add the cake mix and 1 cup water and mix until smooth, about 3 minutes. Fill the muffin liners to just below the rim and bake until puffed and golden, 18 to 20 minutes. Remove from the oven, let cool slightly in the tins, then transfer the cupcakes to a wire rack to cool completely.

Meanwhile, purée the strawberries in a blender or small food processor. Sift the confectioners' sugar and place in a medium bowl. Pour in the strawberry purée and whisk until smooth. Dip the tops of the cooled cupcakes into the strawberry glaze. Let the cupcakes sit for a few minutes for the glaze to firm up, then serve.

Grilled Summer Fruit

Place the fruit on skewers and let your kids sprinkle on the sugar. When you grill the skewers the sugar caramelizes, giving them a nice crunch; but you'll know it's still a very healthy dessert that is mostly fruit. You may use apricots and peaches in place of any of the suggested fruits if you like.

6 servings

Nonstick spray
3 firm but ripe nectarines, halved, pitted
3 firm but ripe purple or black plums, halved, pitted
3 firm but ripe red plums, halved, pitted
3 tablespoons sugar

Special equipment: 6 metal skewers or thick wooden skewers soaked in water 30 minutes

Spray the grill rack with nonstick spray and preheat the grill to medium-high. Thread 1 piece of each fruit onto each of 6 skewers so that the cut sides line up and lie flat. Sprinkle the sugar over the cut sides of the fruit. Let stand until the sugar dissolves, about 10 minutes.

Place the fruit skewers on the grill cut side down. Grill the fruit until it is heated through and caramelized, turning once, about 5 minutes.

Chocolate Chip Pound Cake

A bit of mascarpone in the batter gives this cake just the slightest tang and keeps it moist, making it a good candidate for freezing. I always keep one of these in the freezer and when kids come to visit I pull it out and serve it with some strawberries and chocolate sauce for dipping.

Makes 2 pound cakes

5 ounces unsweetened chocolate, chopped
⅓ cup mascarpone cheese, at room temperature
2¼ cups sugar
1 cup vegetable oil
3 large eggs
1 tablespoon pure vanilla extract
3 cups all-purpose flour
1 teaspoon baking soda
1 teaspoon salt
½ teaspoon baking powder
¾ cup semisweet chocolate chips

Homemade Chocolate Sauce

1 cup semisweet chocolate chips
⅔ cup heavy whipping cream
½ teaspoon pure vanilla extract

Place a rack in the center of the oven and preheat the oven to 325° F. Grease and flour two 9 x 5-inch loaf pans.

In a small saucepan, combine the unsweetened chocolate and 1 cup water. Place over medium-low heat and stir constantly until the chocolate is melted, about 2 minutes. Set aside to cool for 2 minutes, then whisk in the mascarpone until the mixture is smooth.

Beat the sugar, oil, eggs, and vanilla in a large bowl for 30 seconds. Stir in the chocolate-mascarpone mixture. Whisk the flour, baking soda, salt, baking powder, and chocolate chips in a medium bowl. Add the dry ingredients and stir just until blended.

Divide the batter among the prepared pans and bake for 55 to 60 minutes or until a tester inserted into the center of each loaf comes out with no crumbs attached. Cool in the pans for 5 minutes, then turn out onto a wire rack to cool completely. (If you plan to freeze the cakes, wrap them well in aluminum foil once they are completely cool.)

To make the sauce, place the chocolate chips in a small heat-proof bowl. Combine the heavy cream and vanilla extract in a small saucepan and heat over medium-low heat until small bubbles appear at the edges of the pan. Pour the hot cream mixture over the chocolate chips. Stir with a fork until the chocolate is melted and the mixture is smooth.

Drizzle the chocolate sauce over the pound cakes and refrigerate for 15 to 20 minutes to set the chocolate sauce. Return to room temperature before serving.

Italian Ice

I made this with my friend's daughter for a school fund-raiser and it was a huge hit. She helped me crush the ice with a rolling pin, then scooped it up and drizzled on the syrup. We used raspberry because we liked the color, but you can make any flavor you prefer.

Serve these with some of the Mascarpone Mini Cupcakes (page 221) and squares of the Chocolate Chip Pound Cake (page 224) and you have a wonderful dessert party for kids or the makings of a great bake sale.

10 to 12 servings

3 cups raspberry syrup, such as Torani
Zest of 1 lemon
¾ cup freshly squeezed lemon juice
¼ cup finely chopped fresh mint leaves
5 pounds ice (about 6 ice trays)

Combine the syrup, lemon zest, lemon juice, and mint in a small pitcher. Refrigerate until cold.

Working in batches, place the ice in a heavy resealable plastic bag and hit it with a mallet or rolling pin to coarsely crush the ice. Place 2 to 3 cups of crushed ice at a time in a food processor and run the machine until the ice is finely chopped. (You can store the shaved ice in a large resealable plastic bag in the freezer for up to 1 day.)

Place 1½ cups of shaved ice in each serving dish. Pour 3 to 4 tablespoons of the syrup mixture over each scoop of ice and serve immediately.

Menus

KID'S BIRTHDAY PARTY
Mini Calzones
Tomato, Watermelon, and Basil Skewers
Polenta-Crusted Shrimp with Honey Mustard
Mascarpone Mini Cupcakes with Strawberry
    Glaze

APRÈS-SKI
Spiced Americano with Cinnamon Whipped
    Cream
Hearty Tomato Soup with Lemon and
    Rosemary
Croissant Panini
Cornmeal and Rosemary Cake with Balsamic
    Syrup

DINNER PARTY
Fresh Tomato and Goat Cheese Strata with
    Herb Oil
Veal Chop Saltimbocca
Artichoke Gratinata
Citrus Semifreddo

ITALIAN PICNIC
Mediterranean Farro Salad
Artichoke and Tuna Panini with Garbanzo
    Bean Spread
Sweet and Sticky Chicken Drumsticks
Chocolate Hazelnut Biscotti

BRUNCH
Linguine and Prosciutto Frittatas
Berry Strata
Pomegranate and Cranberry Bellinis

GAME DAY
Prosciutto Mozzarella Pinwheels
Curried Chicken Sandwich with Radicchio
    and Pancetta
Tuscan Mushrooms
Orange and Chocolate Zeppole

LADIES' LUNCH
Cantaloupe, Red Onion, and Walnut Salad
Salmon with Puff Pastry and Pesto
Strawberry and Mascarpone Granita

SUMMER BBQ
Fregola Salad with Fresh Citrus and Red
    Onion
Prosciutto Lamb Burgers
Chicken with Balsamic Barbecue Sauce
Grilled Summer Fruit

WINTER COMFORT
Tuscan White Bean and Garlic Soup
Rigatoni with Squash and Prawns
Spicy Parmesan Green Beans and Kale
Chocolate Panna Cotta with Amaretto
    Whipped Cream

COCKTAIL PARTY
Apple and Thyme Martini
Pecorino Crackers
Panini with Chocolate and Brie
Pecorino Romano with Apples and Fig Jam

WEEKNIGHT DINNER
Lamb Ragù with Mint
Broiled Zucchini and Potatoes with Parmesan
    Crust
Ricotta Cappuccino

PASTA BUFFET
Orecchiette with Mini Chicken Meatballs
Baked Orzo with Fontina and Peas
Eggplant Timbale
Orzo-Stuffed Peppers
Amaretti Torta

SUNDAY SUPPER
Lemon Risotto
Turkey Osso Buco
Hazelnut Crunch Cake with Mascarpone
    and Chocolate

ELEGANT VEGETARIAN DINNER
Crispy Smoked Mozzarella with Honey
    and Figs
Asparagus, Artichoke, and Mushroom
    Sauté with Tarragon Vinaigrette
Orzo-Stuffed Peppers
Espresso Chocolate Mousse with Orange
    Mascarpone Whipped Cream

WELCOME SPRING
Prosciutto and Melon Soup
Salmon in Lemon Brodetto with Pea Purée
Pecorino Crackers
Ricotta Orange Pound Cake with
    Strawberries

MOVIE NIGHT
Garlic and Sun-dried Tomato Corn Muffins
Spicy Calamari Stew
Green Salad
Chocolate Chip Pound Cake

FARMER'S MARKET MEAL
Asparagus and Zucchini Crudo
Roman Summer Salad
Whole-Wheat Linguine with Green Beans,
    Ricotta, and Lemon *or* Swordfish Poached
    in Olive Oil with Broccoli Rabe Pesto
Berry Strata

GOOD FOR YOU
Tuscan White Bean and Garlic Soup
Whole-Wheat Spaghetti with Lemon, Basil,
    and Salmon
Grilled Eggplant and Goat Cheese Salad
Fresh fruit

Acknowledgments

For helping to create this cookbook and bringing my recipes to life, I offer my heartfelt thanks to these wonderful and talented people:

To Tina Rupp and her assistant, Elizabeth Drago, a special thanks for all the beautiful photos. Alison Attenborough and her assistant, Mariana Velasquez, and Liza Jernow and her assistant, Rebecca Lurkevich, for making my food look delicious. Karen Panoch for making me glow. Theresa Stastny, Rick Corcoran, Deborah Williams, and Ivone Moutela for all their hard work and brilliant props.

Andy Sheen-Turner and Katrina Norwood, for always being upbeat and positive about testing and retesting recipes. Pam Krauss, my brilliant editor, who inspires me to be a better writer. And many thanks to Rae Umsted and Robin Turk, for making the shoot possible, as well as to Elaine and John Rabuchin, for the use of their lovely home.

To the people in my life who are always looking out for me: Suzanne Gluck, Jon Rosen, Eric Greenspan, and Sandra Tripicchio, without whom I couldn't be in three places at one time!!

Last, to my husband, Todd, for all his support, love, and understanding. It wouldn't have been the same journey without u!

To the Food Network, for giving me the chance to share my love of Italian food and family with sooo many people. Bob Tuschman, who brought me to the Food Network family and who believed in me from the start—many thanks. Irene Wong, who is not only my producer (on *Everyday Italian*) but has become a wonderful friend—thank you for all your hard work and dedication. And a BIG thanks to the *Everyday Italian* team, for all their hard work and for making my job so much fun.

Credits

For their generosity, my appreciation also goes to the following:

Anthropologie
Gourmet Settings
Crate & Barrel
Krups
Le Creuset
LP Laboratorio

Peugeot
Sur la Table
Table Art
Virtu
West Elm
Williams Sonoma

Index

236

238

Index

240